B114154-1 $10—

D1311906

A BATSFORD CENTURY

1. Batsfords in 1893.

A Reconstruction of the Premises at 94 High Holborn
(now destroyed), by Professor Randolph Schwabe

A
BATSFORD CENTURY

The Record of a Hundred Years of
Publishing and Bookselling
1843-1943

EDITED BY

HECTOR BOLITHO

LONDON

B. T. BATSFORD LTD.

15 North Audley Street, W.1
Malvern Wells, Worcestershire

1943

First Published
Autumn 1943

Made and printed
in Great Britain for the Publishers, B. T. Batsford Ltd.
Printed at The Westminster Press, 411a Harrow Road, London, W.9
Illustrations reproduced by L. van Leer & Co., Hounslow
Bound by The Leighton-Straker Bookbinding Co., Willesden

FOREWORD

THE Batsford century falls into six reigns, and, while simple and steady-flowing in itself, has for background the most tremendous and terrifying transformation in humanity's million years' existence. Is it a "story" for anyone outside our immediate circle? My mother, keen-witted and decisive in her ninety-first year, is emphatic in the negative. But the Quennells have shown the clear appeal of the everyday life of ordinary folk, and we should like to take our place with Ralph Jollibody, John Stoutlook, Maud Malkynsmaydin, Cicely Wilkinsdoughter, and the rest of that quiet company to whom England owes much of its solid material achievement. As we trace it farther into the past, it is a tale deep-rooted in the calm English countryside—back from London to Hertford and St. Albans, and thence to Buntingford, Great and Little Munden, Ridge, Shenley and other little places in the lovable farming Hertfordshire landscape, with collaterals by Warwickshire fields and streams, and in the vale country under the Cotswold edge.

The abiding strength of England comes from such sources as these, and from them I derive a lifelong love of the country and a dash of the Saxon disinclination for the town. It is curious that it should be the war that has sent a company of us to work on the green Malvern slopes overlooking the wide Severn-Avon plain. Nevertheless, for all its country origin, the scene is laid throughout in London, where all its actors nearly all their days lived and worked—no stony-hearted stepmother, but a comfortable, friendly, motherly old city, just the place for "middling people". Now it has largely been torn from us by rebuilding and bombs, but we can think lovingly and regretfully of its pleasant ways and industrious, homely folk.

The story is all of "little" people, to whom we may be happy to belong, who have gone their quiet ways in patience and steadfastness. Like them, I am British, business and bourgeois, and intensely and equally proud of all three. I once chose as a school prize Freytag's Soll und Haben. I never finished it, and never shall, but its noble message of the worth and dignity of trade is emphatically needed at the present day. Commerce is not, as some term politics," a dirty business", but the touch of union that knits the whole world kin. Once in the Suk at Marrakeesh in Morocco I chatted long to an Arab leatherworker, and we found that as producers and sellers we had much in *common; we shook hands warmly and parted with mutual understanding and esteem. My father once broke away for good from an old family who spoke of trade disparagingly; now it is the younger generation which is in danger of bondage to snivelling shibboleths and flibbertigibbet phylacteries: that there is something sordid or soiling in producing, buying and selling.*

If our story is set deep in the soil, it is equally rooted in craftsmanship. My little uncle Herbert once sent me as a boy to hunt up an electrotypers' foreman called Tijou, to see if he were akin to the great Jean of that name, master smith to William III, and noblest of ironworkers in England. It is a joy to study the richness of an old textile, to thrill at the tiny, delicate scrollwork of a watch-cock, or become intoxicated over a Wren church interior. We have always been linked with historic work in stone, wood, metal and plaster, and it has been our privilege to discover and illustrate it, and to have met and worked with such modern craftsmen as Starkie Gardner, the ironworker, George Bankart, plaster-worker and plaster-lover, and above all Fred H. Crossley, medievalist, architect, designer, writer, and photographer of lovely work. We have thus been rooted in England and English life, even if we have accepted books from abroad, illustrated the work of many countries and sent our products all over the world.

One author, from whom we parted for good over a difference of one and two-thirds per cent, trumpeted forth that "there is no sentiment in business". He was a schoolmaster, but obviously no psychologist. The war has welded us individualist book-folk into cheerful, comforting fellowship one with another; our many bookseller firms, even our fellow publishers, are not suspicious rivals, but friendly colleagues who delight in doing kindnesses. The publishers especially have found their way to a new wartime solidarity, hitherto unknown in their history. No trade society can have risen more finely to the occasion than the Publishers' Association, under its able leadership, for which our grateful appreciation must be shot with admiration. It has wrestled with complexities, it has coped adequately with every grade of Government Department. Its Economy Agreement is a piece of real planning, a technical achievement of high order. The Association has turned its difficult trade into a real Flying Fortress, powerful to forge ahead and armed at every angle for defence. The continuance of these efforts after the war will be an unmixed blessing. And we should be ungrateful if we failed to pay our affectionate tribute to the memory of Walter Spencer and Herbert Walford, who are gone from us, but long delighted in showing that unselfish helpfulness and a lavish welcome could glow brightly among masses of ancient books and prints.

FOREWORD

Our old friend George Rimell was once called in to give evidence in a print case. "Do you ever make a mistake in judgment?" asked the other side's Counsel. "Very often," replied that most modest man. "That is the proper answer to make," interposed the judge. Certainly this is distinctly applicable to many years of publishing; we cannot be unmindful of failures and shortcomings. If the first sentences of the General Confession are not illuminated on our walls, it is because we have their avowals ever by heart. One writer, in a gallery of imaginary spectres, conjured up a particularly repellent phantom: the Ghost of our Lost Opportunities. Its hauntings are by no means unknown to us.

If there is anything we might have inscribed on our walls it is the one word Ebenezer, even though my friend J. G. Wilson of Bumpus remarked: "If ye say that worrd to any of my staff, they'll tell ye they're not acquainted with the gentleman".* For we have been infinitely helped—turned back from petering-out paths, warded off from precipitous spots, set before wide-opening doors and led into a large place.

In the only sharp exchange my uncles ever had, Herbert many times said to the elder, "I have only four words to say to you, Bradley: Learn to be grateful". We have taken that lesson to heart; we are glad to be grateful in many ways, e.g. to our predecessors, to the pioneers of photography, and especially to a large company of fellow workers: our authors who have laboured with us, some for over thirty years; our staff, keen, patient, intelligent, devoted; and the band of able men in the production industries on which we rely. For to illustrate craftsmanship we must work through craftsmen, the highly skilled and specialized modern equivalents of the old printers and engravers. There are the fine-etcher at the block-maker's, the control hand at the paper-mill, the monotype operator and machine-room overseer at the printer's, the binder's foreman, and a host of others. To them all we tender our thankful appreciation, even though, if gratitude be a lively sense of favours to come, we hope for much more fine work at their hands. Their labours will endure to generations that come after. Even book production has its Benedicite. . . .

HARRY BATSFORD

Malvern Wells
June, 1943

---

* The reference is, it is to be feared, not universally known: *Ebenezer* "Hitherto hath the Lord helped us", 1 Samuel vii, 12.

CONTENTS

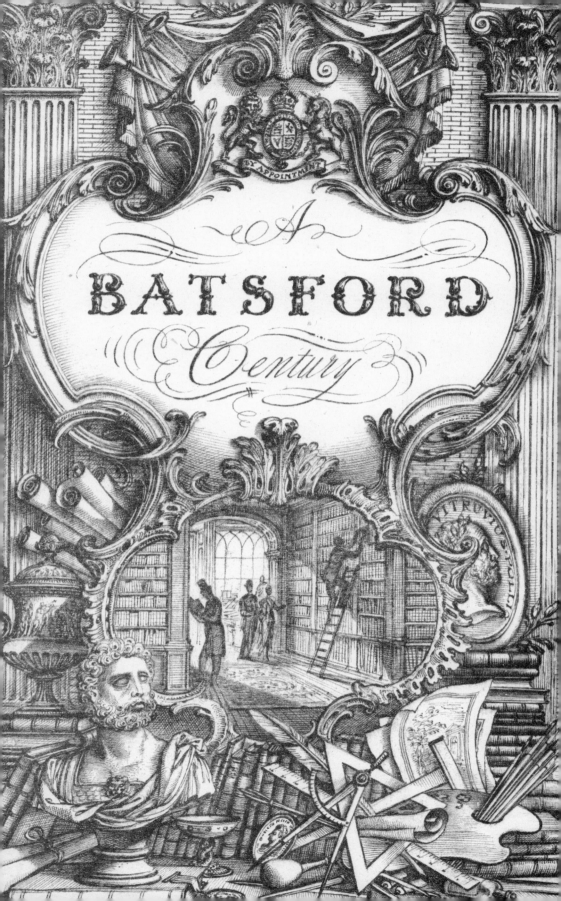

BY APPOINTMENT

A

BATSFORD

Century

VITRUVIUS

A BATSFORD CENTURY

I

In the early 'thirties of the last century a boy in his teens set out from Hertford to join his cousins in London. He doubtless travelled by coach, which would carry him from Hertford through Ware and into the heart of the city . . . near to the house and bookshop of his kinsmen in Leicester Square, where he was to live.

The boy was Bradley Thomas Batsford and his blood was as English as his name. He had lived in Hertford since he was born in 1821, until his parents died and left him to fend for himself. Although he became a Londoner, with his interests deep-rooted in the growing city, he never forgot the county of his boyhood, and when he was an old man, musing on his memories, he would talk of the houses and people, and of the little round-ended Norman Church of St. Leonard, in the hamlet of Bengeo, which adjoined Hertford,

St. Leonard, Bengeo, in 1831. Redrawn by Norah Davenport, after J. C. Buckler.

pronouncing it Benjy, as Hertfordshire men are said to do.

The Batsfords had moved to Hertfordshire in the eighteenth century, from Leamington, where they had a rope-walk. The old gentleman was always very definite on that point, but it looks as if in doing so they were returning to their parent stock, for they had occurred all over central Hertfordshire for three hundred and fifty years. A Batesford held land at "Whethamsted" in 1495, while in the early eighteenth century a Thomas Batsford was a gamekeeper at Great Munden, and at Little Munden there were efforts to prove that Michael Batsford, at the age of nine, was an "idle, disorderly and pilfering boy". There were juvenile delinquents two hundred years ago, but for excuse he was the youngest of a labourer's seven children; perhaps he was hungry.

The name of Batsford is indigenous in Warwickshire also, and in the Cotswolds. When Bradley Thomas Batsford grew older he was able to trace the records of his namesakes—in Shipston-on-Stour churchyard, where their tombstones stand, and at Laverton near Broadway, just under the North Cotswold escarpment, in the parish of Buckland. They must have been sturdy stock who bore his name in the Midlands. He was able to learn of a fine old lady, Fanny Batsford, born in 1837, the year he entered business, who died at St. Mary Bourne at the age of one hundred and two in 1939, and of other members of that parallel family, farmers apparently, established at Buckland Field, the glebe farm belonging to the rector of Buckland. And there were Battesfordes and Battisforths and Batsworths and Batswerks with whom he might have claimed the vague but fascinating kinship which lies in the place names and family names of England and its people.

Every tendril of evidence established the inherent Englishness of Bradley Thomas Batsford. There was the little hamlet of Batsford, with its great house and park on the wooded slopes of the ridge which rises above the valley by Moreton-in-the-Marsh. There were Basford in Nottinghamshire and the small village of Battisford in Suffolk to remind him still further that he was part of the earth on which he was born.

The Batsfords must have been typical of a country town middle-class family in the later eighteenth century. Living at Hertford, they were intimately connected with the equally numerous Bradley family of Ridge, Shenley and St. Albans, whom the Abbey records show to have been established there for some two hundred years. Both families were connected with the two little Hertfordshire towns, for there are two Batsford burials in the Abbey in 1826-27, one of them of Bradley Thomas's infant brother Frederic.

Their father, James, was a tailor, the youngest of thirteen children born between 1766 and 1791, some of whom died quite soon after birth. He married Mary Bradley, daughter of Roger Bradley. He was long established in Back Street, Hertford, now swept away for a car park, and on marrying in 1812 he purchased the freedom of the borough. His children grew up amid mixed neighbourly influences, between the Quaker meeting-house and *The White Lion*. An old doctor's memorandum shows that Bradley Thomas was the fifth of nine children born between 1813 and 1825, and that

Honey Lane: a Street of Old Hertford.
Drawn by F. L. Griggs, R.A.

of his four brothers and four sisters several did not survive infancy. His father died in 1835, and was buried the day after the boy's fourteenth birthday; it must have been shortly after that he set out for Leicester Square. The grandfather, Roger Bradley, died a little later, and as his widow and three children had all predeceased him, his estate of £1,155 was divided among his grandchildren, James Batsford's family. The estate was administered by a young sister, Fanny Batsford—after whom Bradley Thomas named one of his daughters—with John Bickers, and his share of £325 came to him early in 1842, when he came of age, at just the right time to set him up in business as a bookseller.

One possession from those early years touches in a little more fully the background from which young Batsford came, and is a faint sign of the line his interests were to take. It is a tiny selection from Thomas à Kempis, *An Extract of the Christian's Pattern*, edited by John Wesley and published by George Whitefield in the City Road. The little book bears no date, but it must have been published before 1800. On one of the opening pages we read: *Hannah Batsford, her book, and Jane Nodes, died three weeks after being delivered of her seventh child, Novr. 15, 1819. Aged 38. Our loss is her eternal gain.*

At the back of the book is written: *Hannah Batsford. Died May 10 1811. Elizh. Bickers. Died March 27 1819. Aged 43. Jane Nodes. Died Novr. 15 1819. Aged 38. Three Pious Sisters taken from the evil to come.* They were Batsford sisters of the older generation, three of the twelve uncles and aunts; all of the trio died a few years before Bradley was born.

The name from the little book which is important to the story is that of Elizabeth, who had married a man named Bickers. It was to his Bickers cousins that the boy was going on his journey to London.

The Bickers family probably lived above their bookshop and bindery in Leicester Square. There is little from which to write a description of their life, but the few letters and papers which survive give one the impression of a happy, intelligent family with interests and friends which Bradley Thomas Batsford must have shared. Among those friends was Raphael Angelo Turner who, in obedience to his name, was an artist, carver and gilder. He had exhibited at the Incorporated Society of Artists in 1791, when he was a boy of seven. Turner's father, George, an engraver, kept a

2. An engraving by George Turner of a drawing made by Raphael Angelo Turner at the age of seven, in 1790. It was exhibited in the Royal Incorporated Society's Exhibition the next year.

3, 4. Raphael Angelo Turner and Sophia Alexander Turner: engraved portraits by their father, George Turner; both dedicated to Charles James Fox.

5, 6. Photographs of Raphael Angelo
Turner in old age, on the right with a
granddaughter, taken about the time
Bradley Thomas Batsford started in
business.

drawing academy at Charing Cross and engraved his little boy's landscape with portraits of him and his sisters; they are reproduced here (Figs. 2, 3, 4). His decorative trade card, specifying that he held *Evenings for Ladies, and for Gentlemen,* is in the Bedford Collection in the British Museum print room. The trade card, which is reproduced nearby (Fig. 8), gives some notion of the graceful mind of old George Turner, who named his son Raphael Angelo. He, in turn, named his daughter Letitia Josephine.*

One day when the Bickers were out walking in London with Bradley Thomas Batsford—then a boy of about seven—they met the Turners, and Mrs. Bickers pointed to little Letitia and said, "Now, Bradley, here's a little sweetheart for ye. Go ye walk arm in arm with her". The children never forgot their first meeting, and Letitia, who married the boy some fifteen years later, always said that the day marked the beginning of Bradley's determination to marry her when he grew up.

The great buildings of this century make it difficult to stir up any ghosts of a hundred years ago, or to imagine the London in which Bradley Thomas Batsford grew up in the closing years of the reign of William the Fourth. But there is an enchanting little passage which links St. Martin's Lane with New Street, with disused shops of the sort that must have made up the streets in and about Leicester Square in the eighteen-forties. One feels, from the few pieces of evidence which the family papers give, that the boy lived a pleasant life, no doubt reading the books his cousins sold.

When he was sixteen Bradley was formally apprenticed to Henry Bickers, and the document of his indentures (Fig. 7), still in the possession of the family, tells us that he was bound for six years to the "Art or Mystery of Bookselling", and that he was forbidden "to contract matrimony" during that term. So he had to wait for six years before he was able to marry Letitia, to whom his young heart remained constant. The document bears the seal of William the Fourth. A few months after Bradley's apprenticeship began Queen Victoria came to the throne.

As one delves into the stories of old London shopkeepers, Napoleon's gibe becomes a compliment. When Bradley

* The two photographs of Raphael Angelo Turner show him in old age, one nursing a grandchild (Figs. 5, 6).

B*

Thomas Batsford signed his name on the indentures, on March 4th, 1837, he began more than a century of history in bookselling and publishing for his family, who were, and are still, trading under his name to the fourth generation. They were to rise slowly and steadily in material prosperity, placing integrity before gain, and honouring the literature they were to sell and print.

Bradley's indenture, with its blue seal, stipulated that he "his Master faithfully shall serve his Secrets keep his lawful Commands every where gladly do", and not play at any unlawful games. In return his cousins were to give him sufficient meat, drink, clothing and lodging. The part of apprentice was not always happy for a boy one hundred years ago. The versatile Thomas Gent has told of his lurid experiences with a printer. One recalls stories of wretched boys obliged to sleep on piles of brown packing paper beneath the counters, with beetles and rats for company. It is unlikely that the Bickers cousins behaved so callously to Bradley. Indeed, it seems that both parties kept the bargain which they had signed.

Mr. Harry Batsford, the surviving male member of the family, has provided me with a note on the circumstances of bookselling a hundred years ago.

"My grandfather learned all the tricks of the trade from Bickers, whose bookshop survived until a few years ago. Soon after he was apprenticed, he had to do a good deal of 'collecting' for his master. Those were the early days of the first discount controversy. Bickers was an adherent of the discount method of bookselling in the times of the 'ticket' system. The publishers, therefore, boycotted him, to the extent of excluding him from the periodic trade sales, when they offered their books to retailers on 'favourable' terms, an indulgence which, like the terms themselves, would throw a bookseller of to-day into paroxysms of indignation.

"My grandfather used to tell his sons, when they were boys, how he had to lurk about furtively outside Simpkins, the great wholesalers, until after closing hours. Then he would be let in by the back door to collect the books needed by old Bickers for his current orders."

6

II

What architects have failed to efface of old London the bombs of Germany have spoiled since. The generation which is now growing up will never know the joy of our youth in the great city: finding little silent churches in byways; sitting in the cool quiet of a nave whose walls were dark with history; finding Queen Anne houses, unobtrusive and beautifully drawn, almost devoured by the neighbouring monsters of our own century; the startling beauty of Nash's Regent Street and the comfortable conglomeration of "Booksellers' Row" (Holywell Street with Wych Street, Strand), and, of course, Paternoster Row; the chop houses and the musty bars, the little old shops, with the names of their owners painted proudly in gold. Already we see that the war is removing what little the builders left, of all that was old and intimate of the rambling city which we love. It is true that Paris was more elegant, with its distances and avenues, that Edinburgh was and is a city of infinite dignity and beauty, that Vienna was a dream in which the rustle of eighteenth-century skirts was still almost heard, and that Rome cast the spell of centuries upon one. But London, with all its lack of design, its labyrinth of streets and conglomeration of houses, pressed in between gargantuan warehouses, held more beauty for the pedestrian with an enquiring mind and an eye for form than any city in the world. It was the perpetual adventure of all who loved it, and the gravity that fell upon it on Sundays was a strange and lovely experience: when the city, beyond the Strand, took on the quality of an old print, with the pigeons flying across its silent spaces.

But the adventure has already gone. When the wounds of the war have been forgotten and when the ruins are cleared away, a new city as lovely as New York may rise, shining and brilliant. But the men who walk in it will know nothing of the love and beauty which will lie in the dust beneath them.

7

The life that Bradley Thomas Batsford lived in London will be one small part of that dust. The lovely Wren church in which he married Letitia Josephine, St. Andrew's in Holborn, has been bombed. The shop to which he took her as his bride has fallen under the enterprise of someone more ambitious. Theirs isn't a grand story, and it may not be even interesting to those who seek for brilliance and speed. It is the story of an industrious young man and his strong-minded wife, building up a bookselling firm which afterwards prospered, but not until they had struggled for years on the lean returns of a small-scale business. It is the story of modest people who had taste and intelligence, so that their sons became scholarly and enterprising, developing the little shop into a publishing house which has kept its character, that of the publisher-bookseller, for a hundred years. Even the move from the small shop at 94 High Holborn to the fashionable spaces of Mayfair has not spoiled that character or lessened its charm for both author and buyer of books.

I still walk up the stairs of Batsfords, into the dusty untidiness of the house above, to find Harry Batsford cursing one moment, describing a house or a village he loves the next, or dipping into the recesses of his amazing memory, and feel that I am suddenly one with this modest story of his family, beginning, so far as it concerns us, with the day when Bradley Thomas Batsford took his bride to 30 High Holborn one hundred years ago. The shop had an open, unglazed front. A few years later they moved to premises at 52 High Holborn, which they were to occupy for nearly fifty years, until 1893.

Holborn was the booksellers' corner of London. Harry Batsford has told me how his grandfather began business by dealing in general and medical books. There is a small early catalogue of about 1853 which refers to "Bradley Batsford's cheap bookshop, three doors west of Brownlow Street". He was surrounded by twenty other booksellers within a quarter of a mile. But he said in 1895 that only two of them had, like him, survived.

The firm possesses two sales books, bound in vellum, covering about 1843-50, which give some idea of the modesty with which Bradley and Letitia began their business. An early entry, which may be taken as typical, was for May 18th, 1844, when the day's sales were:

7. Bradley Thomas Batsford's Indentures of Apprenticeship
to Henry Bickers, dated March 4th, 1837.

8. George Turner's Decorative Trade-Card for his "Drawing Academy
for Ladies . . . and for Gentlemen", *circa* 1790.
An example is in the Bedford Collection in the British Museum.

9. Holborn Hill in the Eighteen-thirties: from an engraving after T. H. Shepherd. In the background is the tower of St. Andrew's Church, where the Batsfords were married in 1843.

10. Paradise Row, Chelsea (now destroyed), where Letitia Batsford lived as a girl.

From a water-colour by G. Munson.

Land of Burns	1.	0.	0.	4.	0.
Pinnoch	1.	6.		3.	
British Drama					
2 vols.	7.	0.		2.	6.
Mattly Garden	8.	0.		3.	0.
Burden Sermons	1.	6.		8.	
Pilot	1.	8.		10.	
Wilberforce's					
Christianity	1.	6.		6.	
Milton & Coleridge	9.	10.		7.	9.
Ayr		4.		4.	
Evangelical Magazine	1.	0.		1.	0.
Penrich England	1.	6.		3.	

	1. 1. 1.
Sandford & Merton		
Crusoe	5. 0.	2. 1.
		1. 3. 2.
M. Catauld	2. 0.	7.
£3. 0. 10.		1. 3. 9.

The first column of figures represents the actual takings; the second column the profit, which was £1 3s. 9d. for the day. They were not always so fortunate. On May 23rd, when they sold Thornton's *Prayers*, Cooper's *Pilot*, Kitchener on *Economy*, Porter's *Lake of Killarney* and *A Gallery of Portraits*, the profit was only fourteen shillings and twopence.

The names of some of the volumes in those early records give an idea of the books which were in demand during 1844, the prices they brought, and the profits made from them:

Book	Price	Profit
Walker's Dictionary	4/-	9d.
Don Juan	1/-	3d.
Mahon's Europe, 2 vols.	3/6	1/6d.
Bell's 6 vols. Horace	£2/10/-	5/6d.
Burden's Sermons	1/6	8d.
Doddridge's Exposition	12/-	4/-
Byron Giaour's Bride	1/6	4d.
Milton, 6 vols.	£1/-/-	3/4d.
Kirke White	3/-	6d.
Scott's Poetry	1/3	9d.

Book	Price	Profit
Life of Pitt	1/-	6d.
Sturm's Reflections	4/6	2/-
Ovid's Art of Love	1/-	2d.
Zumpt's Grammar	4/6	2/-
Gay Poems	1/-	5d.

We find that *The Remains* of Kirke White, the protégé of Southey, now forgotten, sold a copy almost every day.

The combined sales and day book for 1846 contains, in August-September, the following entries, without the profits being shown:

Whately's Logic	5/-	Malthus' Population	17/-
Brandis' Sophocles	5/-	Wishow's Analysis of Rail-	
Graham's Chemistry	12/-	ways	17/-
Brandes' Dictionary	£1/15/-	Swift's Works	£1/7/-
Booth's Dictionary	6/-	Wilson's Austria	4/-
Lavater's Physiognomy	7/-	Francoeur's Mathematics	5/-
Hind's Arithmetic	1/6	Cooper's Surgical Dictionary	5/-
Cranmer's Works	5/-	De Morgan and Kater's	
Riddle's Latin Dictionary	12/-	Mechanics	5/-
Guyot's Civilisation	2/6	Gibbon's Rome 12th	£1/1/-
Pickwick Papers	7/-	Burnet on Painting	16/-

It must have been a hard and exacting struggle for Bradley and Letitia, especially when their family grew, and with the death of the first son to cast gloom over the young wife, of which a touch stayed with her until she died. She never forgot the leanness of those first days, and sixty years later her family would know that she had touched bottom in one of her occasional fits of depression if she made tearful reference to her early married life: to the years of parsimony and meagre profits on the few secondhand books they sold . . . days when the brightest entry in the sales book was for *Phillips on Indigestion*, 2/6d. Only the earliest account books survive. There are no day-to-day records of the years when the business began to grow, when Bradley and Letitia could no longer squeeze their growing family of children—of whom they had nine—into the rooms upstairs, which they reached by an open ironwork winding circular stair rising from the floor of the shop.

Their first daughter was born in 1845, and they named her Letitia. Their second son, Bradley, was born in the

2/17/8.   7

Nov 29

Port Phillippe ——— 1 . 6   9
Vol of Johnsons Ramblers   6   2½
Noel ——————————   6   2½
London Bridge   2 . 6   1 . 6
Lawrences Lectures   3   6
Ryans Medical Jurisprudence   5 . 6   1 . 6
Herbets Antiquities of Israel   5   2
Edinbgh Calib ——   2 . 6   5
Bains Englena ——   6   3

£ 1 . 7   7 . 1 ½

Nov 30th

E. Calibrary   2 . 6   5
Clerkes Sermons 7 Vols   16   3
Taylors Manual   6   2
Serein   1   6
Lady of the dake   1   4
Old England   2   2
Graves Media   10   3 . 6
Louis Phillippe   13 . 6   2 . 6
Ranke   6   2½
Pley   1½   ½

£ 2 . 12 . 7½   14 . 0

Entries in B. T. Batsford's Day-book for November 29th and 30th,
circa 1845.

following year. He was to become a centre of the Batsford story. His nephew has written of him:

"He had a strong character, a bent towards scholarship, and well-marked natural taste. He entered the business about 1860 after a modest grammar school education which helped to direct his will power and his sensitive taste along the way of success. He was not strong, and asthma and neurasthenia forced him to the seaside for long periods. But he brought imagination and judgment into his father's little shop. Opportunity came through the death in 1862 of one of their friendly rivals, John Weale, father of W. H. James Weale, the antiquary, author of *Divers Works of Early Masters in Ecclesiastical Decoration* and other books. The Batsfords could not afford to buy Weale's stock or his goodwill, and Weale's *Technical Series*, best-sellers in their day, passed to Crosby Lockwood. The *Technical Series*, conscientiously edited and written, is still published in part, although its first volumes appeared more than a century ago.

"Weale had been a great name for engineering and building in the bookselling world, and when the shop was closed customers began to call on the Batsfords and ask for the books with which Weale used to supply them. So Bradley Thomas and his sons sank their savings in architectural and engineering books, of which they afterwards became dealers and publishers in a big way. Now the rooms upstairs were needed for stock, and it is presumed that about that time the growing family moved into their first house. On the first floor of No. 52 were stored the English and foreign, historic and contemporary books on all subjects connected with art and science. In the middle 'sixties they gave up the sale of general books and became specialists. This change-over is reflected in their catalogues issued between 1855 and 1875.

"The first two little catalogues extant were issued about 1852-55; they are uniform in style, crown octavo in size, each of sixteen pages; one is devoted to Medical books, with sections on Homeopathy and Chemistry, and includes 466 items; the other deals with Mathematics, Classics, Botany, Education, etc., and lists 391 books. The next, probably *circa* 1863, the first after the change-over, has increased to demy octavo in size, and with twenty-eight pages has 736 items devoted to Architecture, Civil, Military and Naval Engineering, Chemistry, Geology, Mathematics, Mining, etc. The

CATALOGUE
OF
VALUABLE SECOND HAND BOOKS
RELATING TO
MATHEMATICS, CLASSICS,
BOTANY, EDUCATION,
CHEMISTRY, & NATURAL PHILOSOPHY.
&c., &c.,
ON SALE AT
BRADLEY T. BATSFORD'S
Cheap Book Shop,
52, HIGH HOLBORN, LONDON,
Three doors West of Brownlow Street.

SCIENTIFIC AND OTHER LIBRARIES BOUGHT OR EXCHANGED.

ALL BOOKS WARRANTED PERFECT.

Orders from this Catalogue to the amount of **Five Pounds** sent
Carriage Free.

Money Orders made Payable at the Post Office, High Holborn.

MATHEMATICS AND CLASSICS.

1 ABBATT—Elements of Plain and Spherical Trigonometry, *second edition,* 12mo. *cloth,* 2s.   1836

2 ACCUM'S Elements of Chrystallography, *plates and woodcuts,* 8vo. *bds.* 2s. 6d.   1813

3 ADAMS' Mathematician's Companion, or Tables of Logarithms, from 1 to 10,860, 8vo. 1s.   1796

4 —— An Essay on Vision, 8vo. 1s. 6d.   1789

5 ÆSCHYLUS—Linwood's Lexicon to, *second edition,* 8vo. *cloth,* 7s. published at 12s.   1847

6 ÆSCHYLUS—Prometheus Vinctus, English Notes, by Griffiths, 8vo. *bds.* 3s.   *Oxford.* 1834

7 —— Agamemnon, English Notes by Peile, 8vo. *bds.* 5s. 6d. published at 15s.   1839

8 ÆSCHYLI Eumendides, cum Notis, Linwood, 8vo. *bds.* 4s. 6d.   1844

9 —— Persæ, Notas et Glossarium, Blomfield, *fifth edition,* 8vo. *bds.* 3s. 6d.   1840.

10 —— Septem Contra Thebas, Blomfield, *sixth edition,* 8vo. *bds.* 3s.   1647

11 —— Supplices, recensuit Frederick A. Paley, 8vo. *bds.* 3s.   1844

The Title-page of one of Batsfords' earliest Catalogues
(circa 1852-5).

first dated catalogue is of January 7th, 1865, and relates to Architecture and Engineering; it set the style for those which followed, though Ornament and the Fine Arts make later appearance on the title-page. One of this series runs to close on 1,000 items, and after that the lists are sub-divided and appear separately, one on Architecture and Art and a sister list on Engineering and Science, abstract and applied. It is interesting to see how the title-page typography changes from picturesque Early Victorianism to something like modern types. From 1867 the printing was often carried out by W. Knott of Greville Street, Brooke Street, a firm with whom, father and son, relations were sustained for some sixty years; it is still in existence close to its original habitat.

"In 1874 Batsfords suffered damage from a smouldering fire which destroyed much stock, the set of reference catalogues and the early account books and papers. But a certain number survived or have been replaced."

Meanwhile, the second son, Henry George, born in 1851, must have joined the firm about 1866. Of him his son, Harry Batsford, has written:

"He was of a singularly winning and lovable disposition, and he cheerfully undertook the double burden of the business when his brother was away, ill or recuperating by the sea. Henry also was enterprising. In his spare time he made up sets of first editions of Dickens and other standard works, and collected such eighteenth-century furniture books as Chippendale, Hepplewhite and Sheraton. Henry allowed a certain amount of playfulness to lighten his enterprise. When a German bookseller, notable for his skinflint buying, advertised for a whole range of the works which Henry was collecting, he sent him a series of unsigned postcards, offering the books at ridiculously cheap rates. He greatly enjoyed the Teuton's frantic advertisements in all the trade papers, entreating the unknown dealer to come forward and disclose himself."

The little girl who had taken Bradley's arm had grown up into a strong-minded woman, though she never forgot her early days. She had been married from vanished Hemmings Row, St. Martins-in-the-Fields, but the Turner family dwelling she remembered most was in Paradise Row, Chelsea, which had much of the character of a village street. The Moloch of modern progress has long engulfed it, but records

ESTABLISHED 1843.   June 1867.

BRADLEY THOMAS BATSFORD'S

CATALOGUE

OF

NEW AND SECOND-HAND BOOKS,

ON

ARCHITECTURE, BUILDING, ORNAMENT, AND THE
    FINE ARTS. (Page 1.)

CIVIL AND MECHANICAL ENGINEERING, AND
    SHIPBUILDING. (22.)

CHEMISTRY, GEOLOGY, METALLURGY, AND
    MINING. (34.)

MATHEMATICS, NATURAL PHILOSOPHY, METEO-
    ROLOGY, ETC. (37.)

MISCELLANEOUS SUBJECTS. (39.)

On Sale at the Low Prices affixed, for Cash,

AT

52, HIGH HOLBORN,

LONDON, W.C.

The Title-page of a Batsford Retail Catalogue of 1867.

15

help us to see the pleasantness of quiet, trim, Georgian terrace-houses with their row of dormers and the shady lime trees in front, looking to the river (Fig. 10). Much of the atmosphere of the day is recalled in Mr. Blunt's book, *Paradise Row, a Broken Piece of Old Chelsea*, published in 1906, the year of Letitia's death. It seems that she was happy there, for she always spoke of the Chelsea days with regret and affection.

Letitia Batsford was a great advocate of herbal remedies. She actually took two baths a day and a brisk walk up hill to keep her joints supple. She even liked fresh air, which was a novelty in those stuffy, mid-Victorian days.

In the meantime the Batsfords had moved their home away from Holborn, for a time to Bridge Row, Pimlico, which has also disappeared, thence to the Colney Hatch district, Kentish Town, and Westbourne Park, where they lived in a little post-Regency stucco house afterwards eliminated by a main-line railway.

III

The progress which was changing the face of London was also bringing activity to architects and builders, and to the publishers who provided them with books concerning their professions. In 1876 Batsfords' catalogue of secondhand books carried a notice that the firm was prepared to undertake the publication of works, great and small. So far as can be ascertained, the first book which bears their imprint is J. K. Colling's *English Mediæval Foliage and Coloured Decoration*, issued in 1874. Before the end of the decade they had brought out, among other books, Professor Banister Fletcher's text-book on *Quantities*, a work which is still issued, after sixty-five years, in a vastly enlarged and transformed version. And they had sponsored Lewis F. Day's folio *Instances of Accessory Art*.

The bond between Lewis F. Day and the Batsfords was the beginning of a tradition: a tradition in dealings between author and publisher. It is a strange relationship that grows up between author and publisher: a relationship of temperament and quarrel, loyalty and sentiment. Nowadays publishers are big and grand, catching the American habit of

Established 1843.   June, 1873.

BRADLEY THOMAS BATSFORD'S

CATALOGUE OF

NEW AND SECOND-HAND

English & Foreign Books,

ON

ARCHITECTURE,

BUILDING, ARCHÆOLOGY, ORNAMENT,

THE FINE ARTS, ETC.

On Sale at the prices affixed, for cash, at

52, HIGH HOLBORN,

LONDON, W.C.

Orders from this Catalogue amounting to £3 forwarded carriage
paid to any Railway Station in the United Kingdom.

Post Office Orders should be made payable to

BRADLEY THOMAS BATSFORD, at the Holborn Office.

Cheques may be Crossed "LONDON & WESTMINSTER BANK."

The Title-page of a Batsford Retail Catalogue of 1873.

17

sumptuous offices, splendid directors and communal dinners at which celebrities are floodlit, like film stars. But writing was a humbler trade in the last century, and in fine old houses like Murrays, Macmillans, Chapman and Hall and Batsfords the publisher was usually a scholarly gentleman who was torn between affection for his work and care for his profits. He helped his authors with advice, and he spared the time to tidy their manuscripts and tie their scattered ideas into shape. The bond was real, although it suffered disagreement at times, for both authors and publishers are usually temperamental characters, each imagining the other to be the second fiddle.

There is an amusing print after H. Wigstead, of a bookshop of the eighteenth century, showing author, publisher and buyer against a background of books. It is reproduced opposite. Wigstead shows us a poor cringing author and an opinionated publisher, with a manuscript between them. The buyer, in the background, is oblivious of the human tragedy afoot: the publisher is obviously getting the better of the argument, with aloofness as his weapon.

Lewis F. Day stayed with Batsfords for more than thirty years, to the day of his death. Some of his books are still kept in print and others will be published again after the war. This is a tribute to the soundness of the scholarship of those early writers on design and decorative art, as well as on architecture and building. Even if the houses and edifices of their day are to us overwhelming, their scholarship was solid and their craftsmanship was good.

A detail of the Endpaper designed by Lewis F. Day for his books, with the initials L.F.D. and B.T.B. interlaced and repeated.

Harry Batsford has written: "The relations between Day and my family were of the happiest. They never had a word of written agreement, and Day paid a tribute to that relationship by designing a special endpaper, with the cyphers L.F.D., his own initials, and B.T.B., my grandfather's, interlaced and continuously repeated.

11.   Publisher and Author: from a print after H. Wigstead (1784).

We used the design as an endpaper to all his books, as a symbol of the spirit which should, and which often does, guide the work that author and publisher do together.

"My firm has maintained equally cordial relations with Sir Banister Fletcher, the professor's eldest son, thus keeping alive a family connection now nearly seventy years old."

Harry Batsford has given me a note on the first period of his firm's publishing, which began at the end of the full tide of the Gothic Revival:

"My uncles issued their share of imposing works of 'measured drawings of plans, elevations, sections and details'. But the Renaissance was not forgotten, with Ebbetts' *Decorative Ironwork of the 17th and 18th Centuries* (1879) and Taylor's *Towers and Steeples of Sir Christopher Wren* (1881), with miniature drawings and an excruciatingly elaborate Victorian title-page, reproduced overleaf to give some idea of the taste of the period. D. J. Ebbetts lived until after 1900, and the other author finished up about the same time as Sir Andrew T. Taylor, Chairman of the London County Council.

"In 1882 my father, Henry George, died tragically of typhoid, at the age of 31. The youngest son, Herbert Batsford, the baby of the family, aged 19, then came in to fill the gap. He had been studying to become a barrister, but he cheerfully relinquished the career of his choice, for which he had shown marked ability, to give all his fiery energy to the family business until his death in 1917, after thirty-five years' service. He left his mark on every department he touched.

"It was in the same year, 1882, that Bradley produced *A Grammar of Japanese Ornament and Design* by his friend Thomas W. Cutler, F.R.I.B.A. The art was greatly to the fore at the time, and a number of works of expensive elaboration came out. Though the subject of Japanese ornament and design has very slight artistic interest for us now, and is racially repugnant, the book is worth looking at for its able arrangement, and for the attraction of its lithographic plates in colours, tints and monochrome. It is obviously the result of a sound technical knowledge of production, coupled with considerable taste and judgment. In this same year, 1882, appeared a small folio bound in blue cloth, *The Buildings of Sir Thomas Tresham*, the strange Elizabethan recusant of Northamptonshire, by J. Alfred Gotch, F.S.A., F.R.I.B.A. As with other authors, this book marked the inauguration of

19

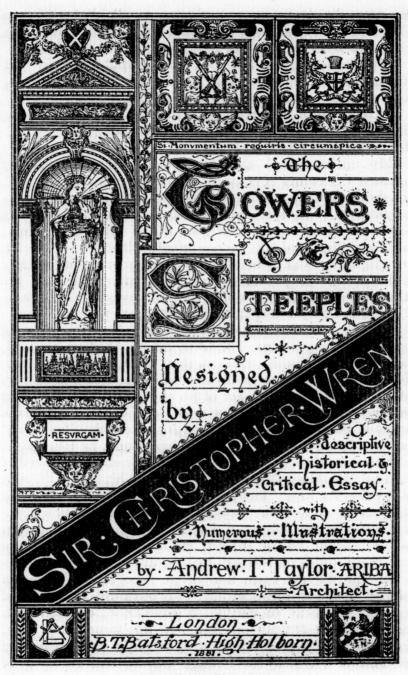

Si · Monumentum · requiris · circumspice ·

The TOWERS & STEEPLES

Designed by

SIR · CHRISTOPHER · WREN

A descriptive historical & critical Essay with Numerous Illustrations

by Andrew T. Taylor ARIBA Architect

RESVRGAM

London
B. T. Batsford · High Holborn
1881

A Batsford Title-page of 1881.

another long relationship between author and publisher. In Gotch's case it continued for fifty-six years, until 1938, three years before he died at the age of 88.

"The retail side of the firm, new and secondhand, continued all this time, actively and steadily. In the eclectic welter of styles of later Victorian days considerable influence was wielded by books of plates, largely the engraved work of the Continent, introduced and distributed by the Batsford firm. To César Daly's *Motifs Historiques d'Architecture et de Sculpture* and his other parallel works of the 'seventies may be ascribed the Gallic façades in Grosvenor Gardens and elsewhere about Victoria; rather later came the Flemish housefronts of the Brompton and Chelsea squares, influenced by pattern books of Netherland architecture, such as Ewerbeck and later Van Ysendyck.

"The early 'eighties saw the inception of the big English architectural sketch books of drawings, measured and sketched, which form so varied and valuable a record of old work at home and abroad. The *Architectural Association Sketch Book* began in 1880, and went into three series, each of twelve yearly volumes, finally ceasing in the last war. The others had a limited issue of a few volumes, produced by the enterprise of the staffs in some prominent architects' offices—the *Spring Gardens Sketch Book*, eight volumes, from Sir George Gilbert Scott's staff; the *Abbey Square Sketch Book*, three volumes, from the office of Douglas and Fordham, Chester; and the *John o' Gaunt Sketch Book*, three volumes, from Paley and Austin's staff, Lancaster.

"The firm played an indirect part in the foundation of the *Spring Gardens Sketch Book*, as Scott's workers at the Spring Gardens office were so impressed by the miserable quality of the draughtsmanship in a book on Belgium and Holland sent on approval from High Holborn that they determined to do better with something of their own.

"My grandfather and uncles always took a particular interest in such out-of-the-way items as these and other architectural sketch books, and in rare and fine works in any way connected with architecture and the decorative and fine arts, and they built up a great and varied stock on all the divisions of these subjects. This may be traced in their catalogues from 1865 up to 1888, when, strangely enough, the firm ceased to issue secondhand catalogues until quite

HYGEIA

DVLCE   DOMVM

The Plumber and Sanitary Houses.

FIFTH EDITION, 1893.

A PRACTICAL TREATISE *on the* PRINCIPLES *of* Internal Plumbing Work, *or the* Best *means for* effectually *excluding* NOXIOUS Gases *from our Houses.*

BY
S. STEVENS HELLYER,

Author of "Lectures on Sanitary Plumbing," *and* "Principles and Practice of Plumbing."

LONDON :
B. T. BATSFORD, 52, HIGH HOLBORN.

(*All rights reserved.*)

A Batsford Title-page of 1893.

22

recently. They sought keenly for the wide range of eighteenth-century English engraved books on Architecture, Decoration and Furniture—Gibbs, Kent, Richardson, Batty Langley among many, and (e.g.) the fine, valuable, three-volume folio of the works of Robert and James Adam, now priced at about £150; and the furniture books, such as Ince and Mayhew's great book of rococo designs, now costing about the same figure. They also enjoyed collecting the splendid eighteenth-century French books of Ornament—Oppenord, Meissonier, Le Pautre, Marot, Delafosse, and the rest of that great and noble company. Occasionally one of these folios in red calf would bear the *fleur-de-lys* of the Royal Arms of France, savagely obliterated in black at the Revolution.

"In 1894 Herbert Batsford read before the Society of Architects a paper on *A Reference Library of Works on Architecture and Decoration,* followed by one in 1897, before the Library Association, on *Reference Works on Ornament and the Decorative Arts.* Both are valuable, for together they form a review of the standard books available just at the onset of modern methods of photographic and colour illustration, which effected so great a transformation in the next twenty years."

IV

Harry Batsford has written a sketch of the day-to-day life of the bookselling and publishing business as he knew it when he first joined the firm, in the last years of the century: the late Victorian days. "The hours were long," he writes, "and the principals worked until eight o'clock every night. The Saturday half-day hovered on the distant horizon, a subversive and destructive innovation in which we indulged only very occasionally. But there was a pleasant, leisurely chattiness about the business life which oiled the running of the wheels.

"All sorts of people would drop into the place and all save pushing, barefaced beggars were welcomed and could stay as long as they wished. They were a mixed and curious crowd: architect customers from the provinces or from London, American architects, who always came in the summer—and, later on, transatlantic publishers, authors and librarians—art-school masters, travellers of every sort and type, printers and binders: the men who wrote the books, the men who made them and the men who bought them.

"I did not realize at first what a cosmopolitan shop it was in which I learned my business. There would be little Japanese, in spectacles, in search of data for the establishment of shipyards and steelworks. I remember publishers coming from Paris and book-people from Leipzig, and an occasional country-house squire who was building up one of the libraries which are such an ornament to the big houses of England.

"My uncles did not look upon interviews as being tiresome or a waste of time, nor did they send many telegrams or live on the end of the telephone wire to do their business. They knew the callers, their tastes and their eccentricities, because they met them all among the bookshelves or sitting over a table. Business was not done quickly. It was personal and leisurely. My grandfather, who would have gone on contentedly with his shop, with the cheap books in boxes outside, was sometimes startled by the bigness of the world opened to him through the enterprise of his sons.

"When I joined the firm he was something of an old character. His will was strong and his eccentricities attractive, in spite of the temper which sometimes burst into flames. I can remember him working at the back of the shop, with my two uncles. They did not use the rooms upstairs except for the clerks and for the growing stock of old books. My elder uncle sat behind a glass screen, from which he would now and then suddenly pop out with lively effect.

"Sometimes there would be a picturesque conjunction of stars, as when old Ferdinand Ongania, the Venetian publisher, appeared and met Phené Spiers, by accident. Then the conversation streamed forth in courtly French, which became more vigorous as their interest grew.

"Ongania's ruling passion was the church of San Marco, to the illustration of which he had devoted his life. His chief work was the many-volumed monograph on it, the greatest ever devoted to a single building, issued at the equivalent of £93 16s. 5d. It was sheer ill-luck that it saw the light just before the general onset of the more recent processes of photographic and colour illustration.

12. Bradley Thomas Batsford: from a photograph
taken in the 'eighties.

13.   Herbert Batsford (1861-1917).

14.   Bradley Batsford
(1846-1906).

15.   Henry George Batsford
(1851-1882).

"Many Germans and Frenchmen used to drop into the shop. There was huge, urbane Ernst Wasmuth of the Markgrafenstrasse in Berlin, and a little, dark, dapper, Jewish publisher, Albert Levy, of Paris, with his finely planned portfolios on Decorative Art. He used to say 'I can sell my books well, dear Monsieur Batsford, in every country except England—and Greece'.

"Uncle Bert would answer, 'Ah, but what do you get in the way of subsidy from the Département des Beaux-Arts, Levy?' and he would retort, 'Oh, I had a pleasant talk with my good friend the Minister, and he offered to contribute ten thousand francs to that book of coloured Japanese textiles'.

"All Uncle Bradley could reply was, 'Well, Levy, do you know what our government does for us? It just filches five copies of every book for nothing'.

"Levy, with the versatility of his race, would be equally ready to make off with all the old engraved French Ornament books, such as Salembier, Du Cerceau, Blondel, and the rest . . . all we could get together for him.

"It is interesting to remember that all these three businesses, Levy in Paris, Wasmuth in Berlin and our own firm in London, have passed to nephews; at least so far as we last knew when we still had links with Europe.

"Publishers nowadays have experts and departments, each specializing in one branch of the trade. During those late Victorian days my grandfather and uncles played every part at the same time. There was little deputizing. Each one turned his hand to anything that came along, dealing with authors, production and advertisement, together with the business arrangements involved . . . sometimes in a way that would now be regarded as wasteful. Bradley wrote all his letters in his own hand, but Herbert exulted in dictation. He seemed to grow in pride and stature whenever he could pour forth words, for a report or a letter. But he never realized his real ambition, which was to go for a long train journey and dictate to a secretary all the way.

"Some of the raw-boned assistants under whom we suffered would not be tolerated in a publishing house to-day. I remember one little Yorkshire tyke, stubborn as his native gritstone, who had a peculiar aptitude for turning the dictation he took down into a jumbled nightmare travesty.

There was a day when Uncle Herbert shook the papers in his hand and said, 'What is this ghastly hogwash you have served up to me?' And the reply, 'It's what ye gave me, sorr'. And Herbert's, 'Do you really mean to say that I dictated that appalling drivel?' And the reply, 'Yes, sorr, I've written it as ye gave it to me'. Then Herbert would flare up and roar 'Then take me to the lunatic asylum. I WANT TO GO'.

"Grandfather Bradley Thomas was growing old. In later years he went home, as a concession to his age, at six o'clock, which was thought to be very early. The brothers would collect their things and get away about half-past eight, a miserable hour to go home in the cold, foggy evenings. They always went to their houses in West Hampstead, where they then lived, in a hansom cab, trotting and jingling through the quiet squares and streets of Marylebone and St. John's Wood.

"The Victorian cabby was an autocratic creature and prone to jog all along Oxford Street to the Marble Arch and then turn up the Edgware Road to Maida Vale. One of them, when told to go 'the shortest way through the squares', bellowed to the uncles, 'Get aht of my keb. I ain't goin' any but the straight road'.

"It was hopeless to try to make him realize that Euclid had anything to do with the shortest way home.

"The fare was 2s. 6d., and the cabby was always given 3s. But Bradley did not mind an argument. Indeed, he enjoyed it, and if one of the cabmen eyed the three shillings and said, 'What's this, guvnor?', he would turn to the argument with relish: 'That is 3s., and if you don't like it, you hand it back and I'll give you your legal fare, which is 2s. 6d.'. If the argument ended with the cabby's hoping that Uncle Brad's supper would choke him, he would jump up the steps into the house, purring with satisfaction.

"I imagine that details of the life which such people led fifty years ago may be of interest. I don't remember that either of my uncles or their wives dined out with friends very often. There were occasional trade dinners and, most delightfully named, there was the *Old Acquaintance Musical Society* to which they belonged. Its concert suppers were held at Ted Burry's restaurant, the Gray's Inn Larder. Most of the men of the circle were keen billiards players, and many of them could sing. Uncle Brad used to tell us of one of them, a tailor, who

26

became bankrupt. At his examination the creditors pressed for 'more'. 'Well, gentlemen,' said the poor fellow, 'I am afraid that I have nothing else for you. But I'll sing you *The Heart Bowed Down* with pleasure if that will give you any satisfaction.' It was the day of fancy-dress parties. The family albums show that even the long hours in High Holborn did not prevent my uncles and aunts from dressing up in fantastic costumes for some of the parties to which they went.

"Old Bradley and Letitia celebrated their diamond wedding in 1903, when the Holborn staff produced an illuminated address. They had lived together in reasonable happiness, but their fundamental differences of temperament had not lessened with the years. My grandfather was humorous to the last; full of quips and jokes which passed over the old lady's head. She received his sallies in silence.

"I can remember the aunts saying, 'But, grandma, don't you see that grandpa has made a joke?'

" 'Oh, has he? Well, I'm not a funny person,' she would calmly assert.

"And my grandfather would bellow, '*Woof, woof, woof.* What a woman you are!'

"His natural sunniness of temperament stayed with him into old age. One day in the shop Uncle Bradley found the old man laughing to himself without any apparent reason.

" 'What are you laughing at?' asked Bradley.

" 'Because I'm so damned happy,' the old chap answered.

"At our family celebrations the younger generation, who loved the old man, and called him Grumps, would always persuade him to wind up the evening by singing the traditional song, 'The Fine Old English Gentleman,' which ran:

I'll sing you a good old song
That was made by a good old pate,
Of a fine old English gentleman
Who had an old estate,
And who kept up his old mansion
At a bountiful old rate,
With a good old porter to relieve
The old poor at the gate.

Chorus, always led by Bradley as the eldest son,—

Like a fine old English gentleman,
One of the olden time,
Like a fine old English gentleman,
One of the olden time.

His hall, so old, was hung around
With pikes and guns and bows
And swords and good old bucklers
That had stood against old foes;
'Twas there 'His Worship' sat in state
In doublet and trunk hose,
And quaff'd his cup of good old sack
To warm his good old nose.
Chorus.

When Winter's cold brought frost and snow
He open'd house to all;

And though threescore and ten his
    years,
He featly led the ball;
Nor was the houseless wanderer
E'er driven from the hall;
For while he feasted all the great,
He ne'er forgot the small.
    Chorus.

But time, though sweet, is strong in
    flight,
And years roll swiftly by:

And Autumn's falling leaves pro-
    claim'd
The old man he must die!
He laid him down right tranquilly,
Gave up his latest sigh;
And mournful stillness reign'd
    around,
And tears bedew'd each eye
For this fine old English gentleman,
One of the olden time.
    Chorus.

"My grandfather's voice was old and a little quavery then,
but it was a happy voice. With the happiness went a fiery
temper which was well known in the book trade, but regarded
with affection and amusement. He was esteemed and
admired by his staff, and always known as 'the Guvnor'. I
think he was really a beloved character wherever books were
made and sold. His virtues were simple. He was upright
without being censorious, quick-tempered without any sign
of malice, and warm-hearted and friendly. For many years
he was a director of a trade benevolent institution, which he
joined in 1851. It was a time when charity was parsimonious
and such institutions were inclined to pile up comfortable
investments and fob off the lame dogs who applied with
scanty weekly pittances. My grandfather fought for the lame
ones with all the warmth of his generous and compassionate
nature.

"Although my uncles built up the publishing and bookselling business beyond anything the old man had planned
when he took Letitia to their little shop in the 'forties, they
never questioned his position, nor did he relinquish his
proprietorship till he was eighty-one years old. Until then
only his signature was valid on a cheque . . . right up to those
last days when, with many objurgations, he would curse the
damned pen as he performed the slow and ceremonious rite
which was the sign of his indispensability.

"The business was assigned to his sons, Bradley and Herbert,
in 1902. Even then the old man would come to the shop,
generally walking from the big house where he lived, in
Abbey Road, Kilburn, through those pleasant old places
of St. John's Wood, Carlton Hill or Clifton Hill, along
Hamilton Terrace (an avenue whose noble dignity and tree-
lined, pleasant spaciousness have never been sufficiently

16. Bradley Thomas and Letitia Batsford: a diamond wedding photograph taken in 1903, a year before his death.

17. Letitia Batsford in Old Age.

18. The Premises at 94 High Holborn (now destroyed).

appreciated), then past the little old Regency church of Emanuel, to the Edgware Road. He knew this walk as well as the stairs of his own house. Then he would go down to High Holborn in one of the coloured horse buses, whose sway had lasted just about the eighty-three years of his life. They began about the time of his birth, and they started to end with his death in 1904, for he died just as the pioneer motor 'Vanguards' were beginning.

"The family tie remained strong after the old man died. We loved our business, with pride and esteem. Even the members of the family who were not in the business cared for it and knew all that we did. I remember my little Aunt Florence during the last war, when we had almost no staff to carry on. She was the youngest of my aunts, and although she was of frail physique she volunteered to act as our traveller in London. It was really a very gallant thing to do. One day she came to the shop of her father's kinsman. The Bickers bookshop had moved to Charles Street off the Haymarket, and there she put down her heavy bag and asked for Mr. Avory, the manager. He was a big elderly man, peppery in temper and a great church lay-worker. She introduced herself, and as Avory was looking over her books he said, 'Well, well. So you are the old chap's youngest daughter, are you? Dear, dear. I suppose you never thought that you would come to this?'

"The poor little lady was quite upset, and we could not persuade her to continue her work when the next season's books came out."

V

"The Jubilee of Batsfords came in 1893, but I don't think the time was marked with any celebrations. It was taken as a sign for more work, because the business had grown beyond the cramped spaces of the old house. They moved a little farther west, to 94 High Holborn, and stayed there for thirty-seven years. Bradley Thomas Batsford had lighted his shop with a lamp and candles in the 'forties. My uncles decided on electric light for the ground floor of the new shop, but they used gas for the rest of the house. There was no longer any hint of the humble book bargains in front of the shop. My uncles got Thomas Harris, F.R.I.B.A., to design the new front of No. 94. The house, which may be seen in Tallis's elevation, was really an adjunct to an imposing classical stucco building, with central pediment and columns, which was built about 1800 for Day and Martin's Blacking (Fig. 40). Like many another pleasant old block, it has recently gone, and No. 94 with it.

"Thomas Harris, who designed the front, and the fittings within, was one of our regular circle of friends. He was an astonishing old man; huge and shaggy, with a big sombrero hat, an unruly beard, a tremendous hooked nose and a booming voice. His laugh was sardonic and his puns persistent and weird. Nowadays I suppose he would be considered a queer oddity. His own day labelled him *impressive*. Facing is a reproduction of the drawing made of him by Raffles Davison. Harris is seen looking into the shop which he designed.

"But those old eccentrics of the Victorian time knew their business, and behind their booming voices and posing was real scholarship. Harris's work and writing were recently thought worthy of two able articles in *The Architectural Review* (October 1942 and January 1943). The writer specially mentioned Harris's somewhat stillborn book, *Three Periods of English Architecture* (1892), and the fact that for a long time there was no copy of it in the R.I.B.A. Library. The mention of Harris's name reminds me of his skirmish with Charles Latham, the lame photographer, also one of the friends of the shop, whom he called, rather unkindly, 'Dot and Carry One'. Latham was a brilliant photographer and took many of the photographs of City churches, country houses and gardens for *Country Life* and for us. His talent went with a red beard and an entire absence of the letter H. Once he went to take photographs of a fine house which had been ruined inside by Victorian meddling. Latham hobbled into the room, stared around and said to the owner, ' 'Ateful and 'ideous. I'm glad I kept my cab'. Then he stumped out.

"Our old friends moved with us to the new shop, and new ones came in, among them a boy from school, William Hanneford-Smith, who has been with us, as junior and then director, for half a century. He came to us in early May 1893. Hanneford-Smith, who still works at his desk 'upstairs',

The Frontage of 94 High Holborn, showing its designer,
Thomas Harris, F.R.I.B.A., looking into the window.
Drawn by T. Raffles Davison (1893).

31

was a son of Francis Smith who worked brilliantly all his life in the publishing firm of Crosby Lockwood, and was the originator of *Kempe's Engineers' Year Book*, Smith's *Tables* and other remarkable works. The work done by William Hanne-ford-Smith has been an integral part of Batsfords' story for fifty years and it will be told in its place as it unfolds (pages 71 to 76).

"There was much of interest then and till recently around High Holborn. Northwards, curious little paved alleyways like Hand Court, and narrow lanes such as Brownlow Street, both lined with shops, led to the spacious early Georgian dignity of Bedford Row and the tree-shaded squares and rows of Gray's Inn, cruelly torn and smashed when London was bombed. There were queer narrow courts and byways which have vanished, like Sarah Gamp's Kingsgate Street. Nearby was a cheap sausage restaurant rejoicing in the name of Orsi & Co., and a greengrocer called Rummans. There was Red Lion Square, with some pleasant old houses which have since disappeared, along with most of Pearson's graceful complex church of St. John. There were two curious alleys which led off the Square; one had all sorts of old book and curio shops, and the other took you from an old Spunging House, past the horrid fascination of cats'-meat places to Lamb's Conduit Street, once fashionable, and on to the vast forecourt-playground of the Foundling Hospital and the restful green peace of Mecklenburgh Square.

"But many of those gracious Bloomsbury squares and terraces have been raped. Queen Square, one of the nicest, had lead cisterns in some of the older basements, but it is now a conglomeration of vast hospitals. Children play shrilly on its paved lower stretch, before St. George's Church, whose painfully Gothicized exterior hides at least the fine modelled ceiling of its Georgian maturity. The north side of the square was never built over, so that the residents could enjoy the view towards Hampstead and Highgate. To it led Devon-shire Street and Old Gloucester Street, with some houses touched with decrepit charm, and from it goes Great Ormond Street, where some of the older door-heads remain as they were in John Wykeham Archer's drawings. But one hospital has not been able to resist the temptation to obliterate by rebuilding the loveliness of Lord Chancellor Thurlow's mansion, with 1709 on the rainwater head,

32

and its delicate ironwork screen.

"Yet we may still rejoice in such squares as Bloomsbury, Woburn, Tavistock, Gordon, Taviton, and especially Bedford, with its many Adam interiors, which has been saved from the intrusion of turning trolley-buses, not by the rotten reed of any official safeguarding, but by the public-spirited organized protest of its inhabitants. No. 1 Bedford Square, designed, with other houses in the square, by the architect Thomas Leverton,* can be surpassed for dignified beauty and restrained charm in few European capitals; 5 and 6 Blooms-

An Old Doorway, now vanished, at Featherstone Buildings, Holborn. Drawn by Roland W. Paul.

bury Square, with Disraeli memories, can well compare with it. The ingenious classic of St. Pancras Church has not been sufficiently appreciated; its delightful Regency vicarage by the Inwoods has given place to a block of offices. But Woburn Walk, a charming if decrepit double row of old shopfronts, also by the Inwoods, still remains close by, though one may tremble for it.

"The fine houses of Theobald's Road have gone or are decayed, but some Georgian or Regency streets still lead off it, two of them connected by Orde Hall Street, one of the ugliest monstrosities ever perpetrated: a study in Victorian crudity of banded blue-grey and red brick."

* The first occupier was Sir Lionel Lyde, from 1781; we meet him in Hertfordshire, where at Ayot St. Lawrence he rebuilt the church in a classic form from the designs of Nicholas Revett in 1788 and was buried there at his death in 1791.

33   E

VI

"There was one pleasant aspect of life in Holborn, among the booksellers. If there was rivalry, it was friendly. I remember how fond we were of the Rimell family, secondhand booksellers and also printsellers. There was old James Rimell, who had founded the firm two years before my grandfather began, and his son George, a pleasant, modest, witty and good-natured man, with a wife who was really a pioneer. She was one of the first women costumiers, with a shop in Bond Street. Her name still survives in the street of fashion.

"The Rimells' place was at 91 Oxford Street, by Dean Street, and my Uncle Herbert loved to drop in on his way to Holborn, to exchange trade gossip and to search their shelves for bargains. With the business link flowed a warm, happy friendship. The Rimells had moved from Maida Vale to Golders Green in 1908, and had built a fine house with a big garden near the West Heath. It was designed by James Carvill, and my sister, Dorothy Batsford, so admired its effect that she got him to design her a cottage which on her marriage was built at Gerrard's Cross.

"By that time Bradley Batsford had begun the publication of big books of photographic plates, reproduced in collotype. This delicate and fickle process was chiefly ours, until the last war, when revised production conditions restricted its use to special books. Gotch's *Architecture of the Renaissance in England*, two folio volumes, had appeared in six parts in 1891-4; G. H. Birch's *London City Churches* followed in 1896. It is sad to realize that the value of that fine record has been enhanced by the recent destruction of many of its subjects. Belcher and Macartney's *Later Renaissance Architecture* came in 1897-1901, a uniform sequel to the Gotch. Those two books were both issued on subscription in six parts at £6 6s. net, and on completion in two half-morocco folio volumes for £8 8s. net. All the plates were photographed specially by Charles Latham on 15 in. x 12 in. plates at £3 10s. an exposure, plus heavy expenses. The enlargement now universally employed was anathema. For some of the City Church interiors Latham

34

gave, with the slow plates of the day, a 24-hour exposure. The ghosts of stray people who sat down and went away may be seen on the plates. The four regional English Cottage books, 1900-12, were similar but on a smaller scale. Some English versions of sterling German manuals, such as Meyer's *Handbook of Ornament* and *Art-smithing*, were successfully arranged, and in 1896 came Anderson's *Architecture of the Renaissance in Italy*, which broke ground as one of the first architectural textbooks to be fully illustrated by photography, reproduced by collotype and also by the half-tone process, which had recently become of general application. It is still in print, after forty-seven years. Professor W. R. Lethaby once came in, and Bradley showed him a copy. 'What a charming little book it is,' said that fervent medievalist, with a sigh, 'but how soul-destroying!'

"Gotch's *Early Renaissance Architecture* followed in 1901. The premature death of W. J. Anderson removed him before the completion of his *Architecture of Greece and Rome*, in the same series; the book was finished by R. Phené Spiers. The firm also tried its hand at the facsimile reproduction of eighteenth-century English design-books, such as Tijou's *Ironwork*, 1897, and Hepplewhite's *Furniture*, the latter just a century after its original appearance at I. & J. Taylor's close by. Chippendale's designs had already been reproduced by Ernst Wasmuth of Berlin, who said of the designer that he 'vos de greatest English mastaire of de Baroque dat evair leeved'. On the decorative side appeared Eleanor Rowe's *French Woodcarvings*, F. A. Crallan's *Gothic Woodcarving* and Emma Phipson's *Choir-stalls and their Carvings*. The latter were drawn, as it was then considered hopeless to try to photograph them. Now we have hundreds of fine negatives of these subjects by Crossley, Clayton and others.

"My Uncle Bradley carried out the preparation of these new books in spite of continuous ill-health. I have a recollection of him working upon them until weakness drove him to some seaside resort. He rarely travelled, except on those journeys. I doubt whether he went farther afield than Welton, in Northamptonshire, where he became engaged, or Bournemouth, the farthest of the seaside places where he tried to mend his health, with the remarkable exception of a mid-winter cruise in 1904 to Moroccan ports in a little 1,500-ton cargo steamer. But Uncle Herbert was more adventurous.

He went several times to exhibitions on the Continent and he liked to range about the English country, buying libraries. In 1901 he went down to Cranborne Chase to buy the books and pictures of General Pitt-Rivers. He was tremendously impressed by the wild Dorset down country, and brought back some amazing tales of the old General. Not until later was it realized that he had achieved lasting fame as the originator of modern excavation technique, nor did anyone understand at the time that the four huge blue and gilt volumes of *Excavations in Cranborne Chase*, of which we handled the remainder, would come to be regarded as a splendid classic.

A Batsford Colophon, designed by George Kruger Gray, *circa* 1918.

"Uncle Bert undoubtedly had a flair for buying. In 1910 he acquired, for £200, the whole material of Newnes' *Collectors' Library*, which was afterwards republished and is still partly in print.

"He also had a talent for turning his associates into friends. Among them was Richard Phené Spiers, Master of the Royal Academy Architectural Schools, who often worked for us. He came from a family as gifted as the Taylors of Ongar (page 104). They were Oxford people. His brother Walter succeeded G. H. Birch as curator of the Soane Museum: a courteous and helpful man who knew how to share his knowledge. Then there was his sister Charlotte, who painted lovely flower studies, some of which are in the museum at South Kensington.

"The uncles had a great regard for Spiers' scholarship. I can remember him coming into the shop and being able to read the titles of the Japanese art books which we imported. He compiled a plate book on the *Orders*, completed Anderson's *Architecture of Greece and Rome*, and edited and wrote many important works, including a re-issue of Vulliamy's

Classic Ornament, printed from the original copper plates a century after its original appearance.

"One link between Batsfords and Spiers had its own touch of regret. About 1900 my Uncle Herbert asked Spiers to undertake a volume of Norman Shaw's architectural work. Shaw thought it all a waste of time, and wrote, 'In a few years they will be saying, "What on earth were these old fogies up to?"' Spiers worked hard upon the book, but Shaw's realism discouraged him and the project was dropped.

The Interior of the Shop at 94 High Holborn.
Drawn by G. M. Ellwood, 1915.

"Many years passed and a new enthusiast came into the field, Sir Reginald Blomfield, who wished to devote a volume to Shaw. He brought us a bound volume of building plates of all Shaw's work, together with a manuscript chronological list, which the R.I.B.A. had lent him. It was pointed out that the collection had been prepared by Phené Spiers, whose crabbed handwriting was unmistakable. He declared it to be 'the most useful thing the old man ever did'. It is just one of those minor romances of publishing. Robert Shaw, eldest son of the architect, made a contribution which helped us to publish the work in 1940, long after Norman Shaw, Herbert Batsford and Phené Spiers were dead. Forty years passed

37

between the inception of the first project and the publication of the book.

"Looking back, I cannot help being proud of my two uncles and of the way in which they shared the work, the scholarship and the attendant prosperity which the business entailed. Uncle Bert lived until he was fifty-six, linking the old days with the new. If we had, or have, any quality as a family, it is that we love England and know England. When old Bradley Thomas travelled up from Hertford to London as a boy he did what many other country boys did after him . . . changed his sphere from the land to the City. But his love remained the same. And my uncles shared that love. I have inherited it and worked to expand it.

"My grandfather, father and uncles worked in their business for three-quarters of a century, and looking back on their labours, I cannot help feeling how hollow and doctrinaire is the present ill-judged and ill-founded agitation on the iniquity of making a profit. The heaping up of gain was not their chief motive. They rejoiced in their work, and it was surely nothing but fitting that it should yield them a modest return. There is no antagonism between profit motive and service motive. All decent producers rejoice in their work and give the public of their best. The greatness of England came from trade expansion, i.e. profits; without commerce we are a tenth-rate power. Away with this inverted snobbishness of anti-trade prejudice.

"In the case of books, and probably of most other articles, the making of profit is the supreme virtue; it is the acid test. If you don't sell your goods and make your profit, the public has weighed you in the balance, you are found wanting, and your firm makes a well-merited exit *via* Carey Street. The publisher's chief preoccupation is to try to meet the public's taste; he can stimulate it and lead it, but to fly in its face means to make a severe loss. This is a very wholesome discipline and it is a definite form of the dictatorship of the people. They pay the piper and we recognize that they must call the tune. When my uncles said that they didn't like a certain style, I used to tell them with the brutal candour of youth that their personal tastes were not so important as what would appeal to their potential readers.

"They would issue books of an expansiveness now denied to us, who by the hard knocks of experience have learned to work to definite quantities and a moderate price, which we dare not overstep. If an author tells us that his inspired writings cannot be condensed, we tell him that our patron saint is Procrustes: the book must fit the bed. One of these gentlemen, for two volumes of a 2/6d. book, produced a manuscript of 80,000 words. Some years later he asked us to reconsider it, and it had grown to 130,000. He could not bring himself to cut it down. And after twenty years he has now gone—it is hoped to a more spacious sphere; but the book will not see the light in this vale of tears."

VII

Harry Batsford's narrative must be broken here, about the time he entered his uncles' business. His own sketch of himself would surely be pale with modesty or distorted through those misconceptions which make us write of our-selves, not as we are but as we might seem to be. So I wish to play writer instead of editor of this story for a few pages in which I hope to describe, and make you like, the man who is the chief keeper of the Batsford tradition to-day. About seven or eight years ago I was asked by his firm to write a book in which about one hundred illustrations were to appear, most of them prints from my own Victorian collection.

The prints were at my house in Essex, and Harry Batsford, whom I had never met, consented to come there and help me choose the illustrations. Up to then all I knew was that he was managing director of his publishing firm. I had no notion of his appearance nor any inkling of what his mind and character would be.

He arrived at Saffron Walden by motor-coach an hour or two early, and travelling with a little of Samuel Pepys' delight over all he saw, and on much the same road as the diarist took when he went to see his patron at Huntingdon, had spent the leisure time in enjoying the landscape and visiting the Saffron Walden museum.

He walked into my house, which is a quiet enough place, with such vitality that one felt the tempo of life change with his approach. He carried some prints and manuscripts which, on the wings of his untidiness, soon became scattered all over the room. My own portfolios of prints might have been leaflets falling from an aircraft by the way they flew about, until I thought I would never be able to entice them back into their cases again. The choosing of the prints was accompanied by an astonishing conversation on the sadness of the parting of the Saffron Walden people with their mazer bowl, on the domestic habits of hedgehogs, the iniquities of the Government, the beauty of the Chilterns and the wickedness of underfeeding cats.

I have met one other man with Harry Batsford's memory and the same grace in presenting its treasures in conversation —Sir Arthur Quiller Couch—the same dancing gift for holding one's attention, so that each fresh recollection comes with the sudden excitement of a card from a conjurer's sleeve: knowledge used only where it is needed and is appropriate, and not exhibited for its own sake. Harry Batsford has a tantalizing gift for reminiscence, ornamented all the way by his affection for people and for the scenes he has enjoyed.

As I listened to him the first time he came to my house, and as the three or four hundred prints flew about the room, like birds in an aviary, a miracle took place on the table. The illustrated pages of a book formed themselves, with complete chronology, complete proportion and balance.

A new publisher is always an exciting prospect to me. For some reason or other authors usually quarrel with their publishers . . . witness the stories of Dickens and his treatment of Chapman and Hall, and Byron's ungraciousness to the Murrays. Perhaps authors grow tired of always being presented at their best, and feel that they can take it out on their publishers with safety. It is a mean trick and advantage, but there it is. For me, my only quarrel with any publisher is when he will not quarrel with me. I love argument and a battle of wills, and it is only when a publisher has been weak with me that I have begun to despise him.

I knew in a flash that there was no weakness in Harry Batsford. Here was a will comparable with my own; a man with whom I could battle, to the good of our mutual pride and the enrichment of our friendship.

There is one more picture necessary to an understanding of this independent gentleman who has less obedience in his spirit than almost anybody I have known. Show him a law and he is "agin" it. Present him with a convention and he tears it to pieces. He is full of young rebellion, but behind that rebellion lies great kindness of heart, the outlook and spirit of a boy, and a love of England which has helped him to remember every lane into which he has turned, every house he has passed, every valley and hill and church he has ever seen. He sets the dull wood of history on fire with his enthusiasm and makes a walk through the London streets into a gay pilgrimage with his knowledge. Didn't somebody write of Dean Stanley of Westminster that the bones of history came to life again under the spell of his knowledge and his tongue? The same may be said of Harry Batsford.

But don't let it be thought that he has no faults. I can enumerate them at as great a length as his virtues. But they are faults that endear him to one, rather than estrange. His untidiness is a positive sin. The chaos of his office quickens my blood into real temper, for I cannot abide the idea of my manuscripts joining such a muddle.

First comes the paper-piled desk. Behind the desk is a bookcase and on the top a hedgehog family in a case, because Mr. Harry likes hedgehogs and was able to buy it for a few shillings. Under the desk is a cat basket, with the door fixed by string; Mr. Harry likes cats and feeds them anywhere. On the mantelpiece are a bronze lion, a few ancient pots from Cyprus, Schwabe's drawing of London from the Thames, some prints and a good deal of dust. Beside the desk is a great knobkerry from Africa—a wooden club two feet long called the Author's Welcome, which Mr. Harry keeps for the recalcitrant, and takes home with him in the blackout, especially when there is a season of robbery in the suburb where he stays when in London, for in wartime he directs the country place at Malvern. What the police would say if they found him wandering through the streets of Golders Green, carrying a gigantic African war club, is more than I can imagine. But I would be among the first to bail him out.

On the table there is the cup of a broken thermos flask, used as a tray into which cigarette ends fall, in dozens. And here sits my friend Harry Batsford, drinking tea, shouting *Hell! Damn and blast!*—yet slowly forming with his authors such friendships that calling upon him becomes a delight. He never ceases to be surprising. The last time I called on him he lifted a copy of *Way Down in Old Kentucky* from the table and asked me to sing it. I obliged, in a bronchial voice, and he listened with polite delight.

I hand the narrative back to him, with the hope that he may be spared to argue with me for many years, since his argument is a greater pleasure than most men's acquiescence.

VIII

"I joined my uncles in the business in 1897, after four years at the City of London School and a brief scholarship stay in Germany.

"By accident I brought one or two interesting literary associations into the shop from my first school: Henley House, Mortimer Road, Kilburn. H. G. Wells had been my science master: a quick-tempered, nervous, slim youth—a missionary in science who had a rare talent as a teacher. Many years after, when I dined with him, he told me a story of those early years, which shows that a science master was an innovation in such a school in the 'eighties. On his arrival at Henley House, Wells had asked the headmaster what was to be done to provide him with apparatus for his laboratory. The headmaster had taken a coin from his pocket, saying, 'Here is a sovereign with which you may buy whatever apparatus you need'. The headmaster of the school was J. Vine Milne, whose son, A. A. Milne, I remember as a little boy with golden curls. Alfred Harmsworth had been founder and first editor of the school magazine before I went to Henley House.

"All this is now forty-six years ago, so I feel that I have become a veteran in the firm of Batsford. It certainly seems a long time since the day when I arrived to work under the eyes of my uncles. The first job I did was to catalogue a collection of papers extracted from some engineering minutes of proceedings. One of these bore the fearsome title, 'Blasting Operations at Hell's Gate'. I thought it quite amusing and showed it to Uncle Herbert, but the joke recoiled on me. He chuckled and said, 'Ah, my boy, you'll get plenty of that here.' Never was truer word spoken.

"The firm has never worked with rigid organization, and like Hanneford-Smith, who was already with the Batsfords, I was put on to every kind of job. We were soon supervising the production of books. Hanneford-Smith's engineering background stood him in good stead in building up and seeing through the press Moore's *Sanitary Engineering*, an encyclopædic affair of masses of cuts. So we simply had to pick up our job. We also took our turn of duty in the shop, learned to list books for an American library subject offer, and replied to enquiries and letters. Or we drafted a publication prospectus, always a Batsford feature. We wrestled with paper merchants, engravers, builders, collotypers, printers and authors, and learned to direct the 'colour' of a half-tone sheet in the roaring machine-room of an Edinburgh printer. I was sent to Surrey to select subjects from the photographs of a postcard firm, and I went to the British Museum or the Victoria and Albert print room to search for engraved illustrations.

"The first independent job of my own creation was to begin a publishing cost record, non-existent before 1900. Gradually a method of costing was worked out so that estimates could be prepared to test the financial soundness of a project. It may seem fantastic, but my uncles had never done this. At least it shows that if they were in some ways casual they could not be termed mercenary.

"The firm learned to commission authors to write books, and I worked, under Uncle Herbert's supervision, on Francis Bond's great work on *Gothic Architecture in England*. By the time the popular series on Houses, Churches, etc., was coming out Hanneford-Smith and I knew how to work with Uncle Herbert.

"I remember a busy time in publishing during those first years. There was the first excitement of seeing a book produced, and the thrill of my first publication appearing. It was Lewis F. Day's *Alphabets Old and New*, and my nephew Brian has recently transformed it, after forty-five years' steady sale, for post-war re-issue. That was my first experience of seeing a manuscript and its illustrations pass through the trinity of crafts—authorship, printing and selling—which gives books to the public. The years 1902-6 were not very productive, but we did come upon one landmark in our story: the publication of Francis Bond's book, which I have mentioned a few lines back. It was an outstanding example of lavish illustration and profuse text, on a scale that these parsimonious days would not permit. So also was Triggs'

Formal Gardens in England and Scotland, a folio of Latham's photographs with drawn plates, brought out by subscription.

"When I joined the firm its character was changing with the times, and the old figures were passing away. In 1904 my grandfather died, a year after he had celebrated his diamond wedding to Letitia. He came to the office almost every day up to the end of 1903, so I was allowed a last glimpse of the life of this fine old man who took many of the ghosts with him when he died. Less than two years later my eldest uncle died, after forty-five years of continuous service. The publishing side of the business had been his creation, and in his time it had made the secondhand book business take lower place, Then my grandmother died. So we came to 1907 and to more changes in our fashion.

"My Uncle Herbert aimed at appealing to the general public with a series of well-illustrated popular text-books on the English House, Cathedral, Parish Church, Village and Manor House. I think he was right. Beauty was no longer merely the privilege of the few, and the average Englishman was beginning to care for the story of his island and the buildings on it.

"Uncle Herbert opened with a two-volume folio on Tudor Domestic Architecture begun by Thomas Garner and completed by Arthur Stratton, 1907-11. This work formed one of a uniform trio with those on the later styles by Gotch, and Belcher and Macartney. The first of the text-books was *The Growth of the English House* by J. Alfred Gotch. It is still known as Gotch's *Growth*. One day Uncle Herbert dashed into a provincial library and asked, 'Have you got Gotch's *Growth?*' The librarian happened to be a confirmed invalid and said that it was practically the only ailment he hadn't got.

"Uncle Herbert took up these fresh developments with eagerness, and during the eight years between 1906 and the beginning of the last war he was extremely active, here and abroad. He exhibited books at the Brussels Exhibition; he travelled; he photographed buildings; he lectured; and he engaged in research in libraries and museums all over the country. Herbert's days in research were not wasted. He found the original drawings by J. A. du Cerceau, incorporated in Ward's *French Châteaux and Gardens*, while searching in the British Museum, and he discovered the original oil

THE DOMESTIC ARCHITECTURE OF ENGLAND DURING

THE TUDOR PERIOD

Illustrated in a series of Photographs &
Measured Drawings of Country Mansions
Manor Houses and smaller buildings
With Historical and Descriptive Text

by

THOMAS GARNER

and

ARTHUR STRATTON

Volume One

LONDON

B.T. BATSFORD, 94, HIGH HOLBORN

MCMXI

The Title-page of Garner and Stratton's *Tudor Architecture*, engraved on
wood by Percy Smith (1911), who did much of the decorative
lettering for the firm.

painting of Robert Adam by Zoffany at Blair Adam, on his visit there, when he was preparing Swarbrick's book on the Adam Brothers. Some time after, the picture appeared in a London auction room as 'a portrait of a gentleman'. Uncle Bert recognized it and bought it; it has since been added to the National Portrait Gallery.   To him also was due the discovery of an unknown earlier state of Piranesi's *Carceri*— those strange, gloomy, imaginative etchings of vast imaginary dungeons—while preparing the monograph on the great Roman etcher by his friend Arthur Michael Samuel, later Lord Mancroft.

"But Herbert's greatest discovery was the century or more of volumes of Buckler drawings, thousands of sensitive sketches of England's architectural riches, largely destroyed. Many of them have been reproduced, but far more remain to be given to the public—if they are sufficiently interested.

"I often wonder where this appetite for scholarship in the Batsfords came from. I don't think that Bradley Thomas brought it with him from Hertford. Perhaps it was old Raphael Angelo Turner, through his own disappointment as an artist, handing on something to us through Letitia. I always imagine that the old man was a great artist in his heart, with just that lag in talent which kept him away from marked success. I do not know, but I suspect that the chief reason why Bradley and then Herbert buried their noses in books, why I share their love, and why my nephew, Brian Cook, is an artist, is because of some persistent strain of the artist in my grandmother's family, rather than the more sturdy stock which came up from Hertford with my grandfather.

"As he grew older, Uncle Herbert was gripped by a love for the beauty of old craftsmanship that amounted to a passion. It displayed itself in the broadest catholic spirit. I remember how he admired Regency work at the time when it was regarded very lightly. He planned a wide series of volumes on the various aspects of the crafts. Hundreds of photographs were taken and editors were engaged. I really do not think that Uncle Herbert thought of money first. He was astute enough not to run blindly into disaster, but I believe that pleasure and profit lived amicably together in his enterprises. But this one great enterprise was guillotined for good by the last war. Uncle Herbert had a special affection for the furniture and fittings of the Wren churches in the City, and he had scores of them recorded by the photographers he engaged. He had taken a high, many-storied warehouse in Gate Street, Lincoln's Inn Fields, and the craftsmanship material, its boxes, portfolios, negatives and drawings, was spread all over it. He was a plunger, and he gave full vent to his propensity over those records of the Wren churches for the Craft series. The collection was not made as a purely business venture, but the chance came to use a selection of the photographs in illustrating Gerald Cobb's *Old Churches of London*, published in 1942. This book is really a memorial to Uncle Herbert's affection, as well as to the buildings, of which so many have since become burnt offerings on the altar of National Socialism.

"The firm made an interesting but unsuccessful experiment about this time. In 1911 we began to publish a series of eighteen *Fellowship Books*. The subjects were what we vaguely describe as abstract—Friendship, Solitude, Romance and others. They could not have been more carefully written or produced with greater taste. They still are charming little books, to hold and to read. There were no illustrations—an innovation for us. But the *Fellowship Books* fell on an ungrateful world, for the abstract was not appreciated. So Uncle Herbert left it alone after that.

"In 1912 he published Vallance's *Old Colleges of Oxford*, an outstanding book; the title-pages are reproduced on the next two pages. Then came Professor Richardson's *Monumental Classic Architecture*, a bible of Regency and Early Victorian public buildings, and a noble book. On the day that the Germans entered Bruges we published Wade and Stratton's *Bruges*.

"We were a family business and families sometimes fall out. By 1913 the affairs with Bradley Batsford's representatives had reached an inevitable deadlock. The details do not matter, but it was clear that something had to be done. We found a friend to help us in Lord Leverhulme, then William Hesketh Lever. Uncle Herbert was helping him to build up his remarkable architectural library. Among his possessions bought from us were Sydney Jones' original drawings of English villages and manor-houses, but these were burned in a fire in his country house. The little man, who always spoke with a strong Lancashire accent, was extremely deaf. I

47

The Decorative Frontispiece of Vallance's *Old Colleges of Oxford* (1912).
Drawn by Harold Nelson.

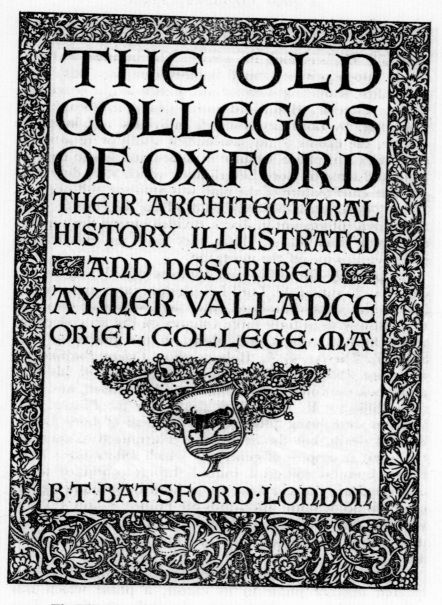

THE OLD
COLLEGES
OF OXFORD
THEIR ARCHITECTURAL
HISTORY ILLUSTRATED
AND DESCRIBED
AYMER VALLANCE
ORIEL COLLEGE · M·A·

B·T·BATSFORD·LONDON

The Title-page of Vallance's *Old Colleges of Oxford* (1912).
Drawn by Harold Nelson.

remember that he often listened with his hand curled over his ear.

"Uncle Herbert took his advice. The business was converted into a private limited liability company, with himself as first managing director and myself as the other permanent director. Hanneford-Smith joined the board very soon after. By Lord Leverhulme's individual and ingenious scheme, the claims of my late uncle's family were satisfied, partly in cash, plus a balance in debentures (some held by them and some by Lord Leverhulme) which were duly paid off. The chief feature of the plan was amusing and original. For any debentures that were paid off the directors received the equivalent amount in shares, divided among them in any proportion they chose. Thus they had an encouraging incentive to wipe off the mortgage.

"Apparently friendship and business mixed well in this case, for, to anticipate, Lord Leverhulme came more closely into the interests of the firm. After the last war he arranged to publish with us three large volumes on the art collections which he had bought and placed in the gallery at Port Sunlight. The late R. L. Hobson edited *Chinese Porcelain and Wedgwood Pottery*, the late Percy McQuoid and his wife undertook the volume on *Furniture and Embroideries*, and after some difficulty R. R. Tatlock dealt with the *Pictures*. The volumes were being produced at the time of Lord Leverhulme's death, but the firm of Lever arranged to continue the work, in a spirit of generosity which softens one's heart to big business concerns. Indeed, Levers continued to be connected with us as a firm, for in Lord Leverhulme's place came his accountant, afterwards Sir Francis d'Arcy Cooper, who became chairman of Levers, the greatest commercial undertaking in the world. In Sir Francis we found a friend and adviser.

"So, with a new and ably devised constitution, Batsfords entered another phase in its career, a phase which was influenced eight months later by the outbreak of war. Two years after came the death of Uncle Herbert, on January 14th, 1917.

"When Herbert Batsford died, his close friend, Professor A. E. Richardson, wrote of him in *The Journal of the Royal Institute of British Architects:*

'His was a career of extraordinary moment to the architectural profession, for his characteristics were unique in resembling those associated with the eighteenth-century publishers, who combined the functions of editor and patron and encouraged architects to record their own impressions of the meaning of architecture.

'It is no light task to pen one's thoughts of a friend whose knowledge and enthusiasm inspired respect from all he came into touch with; he was a lineal and apostolic descendant of that remarkable group of men who published a century and a half ago from positions in High Holborn within a hundred yards of the same spot.

'From 1891 to the present day, the firm of Batsford has been associated with the majority of the modern works in architecture, ranging from Mr. Gotch's folios, Messrs. Belcher & Macartney's later Renaissance examples, Mr. Stratton's Tudor architecture, and Mr. Ward's treatise on the Renaissance in France. It is noteworthy that the whole series of volumes on architecture produced in England are the result of private enterprise, and this is in marked contrast to the excellent system that pertains in France, where the Ministry of Fine Art has lent its support to recording the national monuments.

'Herbert Batsford soon realized that new methods were required if architects and the general public were to benefit from the study of books, and his immediate activities date from the start of the century, and this policy was continued more vigorously after the father's death. There can be no denying the fact that Herbert Batsford was an enthusiast, not, however, of the dangerous type who rush headlong after the latest fashion, but a genius who carefully weighed the possibilities of a book, and looked upon it primarily from the point of view of the requirements of the practising architect. He knew his audience, and encouraged those who came to him with immature ideas to spare no pains to produce the best results obtainable.

'His knowledge of books was remarkable; he seldom had recourse to catalogues or library lists; what he did not at first fully understand he made it his business to master, and astonished the majority of his friends with his vast knowledge of the atmosphere of the past. He had a passion amounting almost to an obsession for the works of the eighteenth century, and rare taste and discrimination as well as a minute knowledge of the prints, mezzotints, and engravings produced during the past three hundred years. His study of ornament and craftsmanship was founded on keen artistic perception, with admiration amounting to reverence for the works of real artists. The contents of every library and museum of importance in the country were known to him, and his vivacious figure was frequently to be seen in the print room at the British Museum as well as at Kensington.

'As a student of London, Herbert Batsford had few equals; all the aspects of London life in the past made an especial appeal to his receptive and sensitive temperament: he studied with care all that could be learned from bygone customs, and as his knowledge widened he responded more keenly to the teachings of history. In addition to his study of the Metropolis, nearly every place of importance in the Kingdom was visited. Those who accompanied him on his travels know the almost boyish enthusiasm he expressed for fine work of every description.

'Herbert Batsford had no sympathy with small policies: he demanded books from his authors of large scale, apart from size. His delight was in books, fine books, rare books, new books—and yet again books, a factor which prompted him to publish the "Fellowship Series", edited by Mrs. Arthur Stratton. In the advancement of taste he played a very noble part, and if at times his attitude was didactic he more than atoned for it by the confidence he inspired among those who had the good fortune to be under his direction.

'Herbert Batsford was more than an ordinary publisher, he was primarily a patron of the arts, and did more than most men to strengthen the position of architects with the public. It required courage to finance ventures without a government subsidy, but it was rare for him to make a mistake, and the series of volumes bearing the name of the firm carry the impress of taste and distinction for the inspiration of posterity.' "

IX

The records of Batsfords during the last war suffer because the staff was so small that nobody found time to write down very much. Hanneford-Smith and A. J. Green, the chief accountant, were the only ones of the permanent staff who were not drawn into the Services. The former was at his desk every day during the war and did not allow the work of the firm to fall away. Harry Batsford went to the Aeronautical Inspection Directorate, and later became a Captain in the R.A.F. He was able to stay in London for all of the time and thus keep half an eye on the business. Some idea of the family pride which held the Batsfords to their business is gained from the story of his sister, Dorothy Alice Cook, then married, going to the shop each day and wrestling with the accounts, and with the female staff; an innovation which would have horrified old Bradley and Herbert.

With all the muddle and depletions of war, the firm still published a fair number of books. There was a work on Robert and James Adam, and Crossley's *English Church Woodwork*, the first of a Church Art Series. As a casual experiment, Batsfords published their first country book: the forerunner of what was to be the greatest tide of their success. This was E. C. Pulbrook's *The English Countryside*. It was also the first Batsford book with a coloured wrapper . . . another innovation for the times. Harry Batsford has noted that the wrapper was done "by that breezy, able designer-friend, Fred Taylor, who obligingly supplied us with his drawing for a fiver".

Early in 1914, before the war began, Batsfords had been asked to look at an enormous amount of material which had been collected by "that strange, original, versatile genius" Colonel H. H. Mulliner, who was a gun-mounting fan, a furniture collector and Autolycus purchaser of all kinds of businesses. Batsfords gave him £900 for the rights and all the hundreds of blocks of a work which was published as *The Library of Decorative Art*, one of their most important productions. This comprised Francis Lenygon's *Decoration in England*, 1640-1760, and *Furniture in England*, covering the same dates. There was also *English Tapestry* by W. G. Thomson.

Harry Batsford has given me a note on these and the other books which were brought out among the difficulties of war. He has written: " 'Lenygon'* was really Colonel Mulliner and Margaret Jourdain. Colonel Mulliner had collected and arranged myriads of photographic plates covering decoration and furniture from 1640 to 1760, in conjunction with Margaret Jourdain, who supplied the text. After the war she joined the firm in producing complementary volumes on *The Early Renaissance* and *The Later Classic Revival*, thus arranging the series as a quartet, covering the whole Renaissance period from 1500 to 1820. Another author who was not dismayed by the war was Gotch, who contributed a sequel to his *Early Renaissance Architecture*—a comprehensive volume on *The English Home from Charles II to George IV*, incorporating much original research on the drawings and designs of Inigo Jones and John Webb.

*Actually there was an F. H. Lenygon who directed the American side of the decorating firm; he has recently died.

"This book produced an amusing exchange between Lawrence Weaver of *Country Life* and ourselves. Weaver, assuming the part of godmother to all English culture, opened the ball with a threatening letter objecting to our use of the phrase *English Home* in the title, because they had already used something near it. We replied that we never took any notice of threats, and we went ahead with the book. There was a little skirmishing which ended in amiable settlement. It was rather like our skirmish with Sir Reginald Blomfield . . . a skirmish which ended in friendship. The story is told elsewhere in this book (page 129).

"I look back on the last war rather sadly, for when it ended many of our friends did not come back: the two collectors for the firm, Lewis, who died in London of wounds with the Lord's Prayer on his lips, and stolid Mole, who fell at High Wood on the Somme; also scholarly Claud Green, our cataloguer, who wrote pamphlets in connection with the Church and Finance. Our big, rough-hewn packer and store-keeper, Cox, died from the intestinal trouble the war had given him. And William Henry Ward, author of *French Renaissance Architecture*, died a few years after because of what he suffered. He had been sent to Italy where, as an R.T.O., at the age of fifty, he had talked to the Italian officers on Dante, in their own language. Yes, we lost many friends. Baker, of our retail department, was a prisoner of war in Germany. He died afterwards. Green, still with us, had an army career of only one day. They sent him home. But I recollect him often working at the top of the house in High Holborn, alone with his books, with the Zeppelins scattering bombs about him.

"With all this going on we continued to produce books. Just before the Armistice we began one of the most romantic projects in our story . . . the volumes of Marjorie and C. H. B. Quennell, mother and father of Peter Quennell. They began with *A History of Everyday Things in England, 1066-1499*. It was a book of talks and drawings by artist and architect, for their children. The Quennells had the rare gift of being able to write for children without talking down to them. The book was a great success and a second volume, covering the same subject from 1500-1800, came out in 1919. Then came volumes until all the years were covered, down to the present time, from the Old Stone Age.

"I think these books have been a real and helpful influence on the young British mind. They have sold in thousands and, after a quarter of a century, we still print and sell them. I don't know exactly where their rare quality lay. One is instinctively aware of a simplicity of mind and a goodness of heart in their approach to the everyday things. The books don't depend upon the ermine of princes or the lofty turrets of castles for their romance. They go into the houses . . . the generations of houses . . . and take up the things which the people used and the simple life behind them. They tell the history of England in domestic objects . . . in their evolution, from the crude possessions of the peasants of the Norman days.

"It is part of our contemporary pleasure as a firm that while we are still selling the books of Marjorie and C. H. B. Quennell to each succeeding generation, we also publish books by Peter Quennell, their son, who, I cannot help feeling, is one of the best writers of English prose alive to-day."

X

"There is one figure from those early days I have neglected so far, Liz. I have written of the Englishness of our business. The people who have worked for us have been equally English, and my record would have a gap in it if I did not write of Eliza Murphy, our charwoman, whose name had nothing to do with the fact that she was Suffolk, through and through.

"There was no formal respect in Liz's make-up, but there was great affection. Perhaps the best story to show how she used to deal with us is that of the arrival of Charles Fry, then a fair-haired youth, in 1924. Charles was later to become our director colleague, and I believe that he has taken on a great deal of the Batsford character in the years between. Now he is a young middle-aged figure, with a pair of spectacles worn awry, a gift for fiery anger which trumpets through the house, a chirping sort of wit and great knowledge of his business. But he was a boy when he came to us in the 'twenties, and he must have been abashed on that April morning when he knocked at the door, to begin his duties. He will tell us the story in his own words a little later.

"How old she was I could never tell. Liz was with us in Holborn for over thirty years. She never left the district except for a rare visit to Lea Bridge which she thought 'lovely'. She knew every court and alley in Holborn, but she could never be persuaded to go into the British Museum. It irked her to be called Irish, which she was only in her married name. Then would come a protest in favour of her county. 'It's Suffolk I come from, my dear, silly Suffolk,' she would say. Her father had been a gamekeeper in the 'Garden of Suffolk', between Darsham and Yoxford. But she had an Irishwoman's gift for invention. She would tell everybody, most circumstantially, that my mother had brought me to her when I entered the business, as a boy of seventeen, saying 'Here's my little boy, Mrs. Murphy. I know you'll take care of him'.

"It was pure imagination, but she assumed the part of mother to all of us, especially young Charles Fry. There was more than a touch of Rabelais about her humour and she was a genius at shopping. 'I got 'em in Lamb's Conduck Street, my dear.' Or she got them in 'The Lane', the market of stalls in Leather Lane. She had a Malaprop genius for garbling names; for her, till the end, Lucarotti, our publishing manager, was Jerosko.

"I am not tidy by nature and I have always seemed to be followed by a bogey of papers and books. One day when she found my office ankle deep in cleared-up papers she was heard to mutter, 'The little sod. I'll be 'ung for 'im yet'.

"Liz had a son whom we tried to coax into the ways of business. But, as she said, ' 'e ain't no scholard, yer see', and we had to forsake the experiment. After his death she lived with some grandchildren in what she called a 'bunjalow cave'. It was in one of the Regency streets off Theobalds Road. When you had hammered the people into letting you in, you crossed an old stone-paved courtyard, shaded by giant plane trees, to a low, yellow-plastered building of about 1730. It was half garden house and half shed. Here Liz dwelt in peace and comfort until some obnoxious Overcrowding Act turned her out.

"I could write a book about Liz and her shrewd, bawdy comments and her great heart, which embraced us all. I feel that Batsfords meant as much to her as her own children and grandchildren. It was of one of us that she spoke with her dying breath. She had been the slave of Charles Fry, although she always peppered her attentions with abusive little asides. But affection conquered in the end. 'We all love Charlie,' she cried, the moment before she died."

XI

" 'Charlie,' of course, was Charles Fry, who joined us in April of 1924 and who is with us still, as fellow-worker and friend. But let him tell the story of his arrival at No. 94 and his first glimpse of Liz:

" 'I had been once before into the first-floor room at 94 High Holborn—a room I now remember better than any I have known—to be interviewed for my job with Batsfords. It was agreed that I should come into the firm as Harry Batsford's personal assistant, and I was told to make my appearance on the following Monday morning. I remember the day and the date well, because it was my twenty-first birthday—April 28th, 1924.

" 'Harry Batsford had told me, with typical optimism, that office hours were from 9 until 6.30. I arrived on the corner of Holborn and Southampton Row at five to nine, and stood, eyeing the clock, till the minute-hand touched the hour. Then, rather uneasily, I made my way up the street to 94. The frontage was barricaded by a fireproof shutter.

" 'I rang the bell: no answer (as a matter of fact, as I discovered later, no one arrived much before 9.30, and the most popular hour was towards 10. One of the nicer things about Batsfords was that you could generally do your work in your own way and in your own time—provided it got done. If the staff were never scrupulously early arrivals, few of them, in those days, left much before seven).

" 'After I had rung the bell three times I was aware of a shuffle of feet behind the shutter. The wicket door opened, and I was confronted by an elderly crone, whose sparse wisps of grey hair haloed an incredibly lined and battered face. A ruined mouth produced an unholy, but rather lovable, leer. "Come in, ducks," said a cracked, hoarse voice, "Mr.

'Arry's not 'ere yet". Then, in a sort of aside like an expecto-ration, " 'E's out with some bird, I suppose".

" 'This was Mrs. Murphy, and that was the sort of libel she always flung at us. It was in her company that I was to spend the first few minutes of each of my working days for the next seven years or so, and I got to know much about the Holborn district and the life of its poor from her conversation as she moved about the room, occasionally bestowing a whack with her duster on a book or a chair. Her great delight was to do our small shopping for us, and to buy our cigarettes; and for ten years the stubs from my ash-tray were presented to a similarly battered male acquaintance of hers, "for", as she put it, "the old man to fill his pipe with".

" 'It was a singularly pleasant room, if never a very tidy one, particularly in summer, when the sun slanted into it above the wire-gauze that screened the lower windows, and gilded the dust particles generated by the rows of old quarto and folio volumes that lined it from floor to ceiling. Above all, it was a marvellous room to work in. Those still were the great days of "sumptuous volumes devoted to architecture and the allied arts", and here all around me was one of the most unique collections of these standard works in existence. I was a bit shocked at first by the way the volumes were heaved out, and tagged with slips, or even "marked up" in pencil for the engraver. But I soon became used to it, and flung them about with the best. As a matter of fact, those old books were so tough of fibre that they seldom came to any harm. Here, in the first-floor room at 94, I made my first acquaintance with these famous books and the subjects they dealt with, absorbing something of their knowledge literally "through the pores", together with much of the black dust their calf bindings so liberally generated. Indeed, for those first ten years, except for a brief earlier course of instruction in naval engineering workshops, I doubt if I have ever been so consistently grimed by the end of the day.

" 'The other rooms in 94, though used as offices, were also stockrooms and similarly piled with books from floor to ceiling. The capacity of that old house was really incredible in the way of stocks and people. Once one realized the "point" of what one was doing, one's working hours were gay, uncon-ventional and wildly interesting. It is strange to look back and realize that one has worked for an unconventional firm

19. The Interior of the Shop at 94 High Holborn.

20. The Directors' Room on the First Floor of 94 High Holborn.

21.   Harry Batsford.

all one's working life. I tremble to think of what might have happened and into what ruts I might have wandered but for the accident that took me into Harry Batsford's office, almost twenty years ago.

" 'One of the most reassuring aspects of our office life is that all the directors of the firm know how to lose their tempers. I don't think any of us ever goes home with a grudge or a sense of wrong. We all let ourselves go and, when working at high pressure, we have had some tremendous tiffs, with explosions of highly coloured language all round. Mrs. Murphy probably held the record for these. Nobody could say she was repressed. Harry Batsford came a good second and even I may now count myself a proven third.' "

XII

Women took a permanent place on the staff of Batsfords after the last war. And some of the older men left and opened bookshops of their own. But the character of the business remained, and in 1920 it published Chancellor's *XVIIIth Century in London* and Stratton's *English Interior*, both distinguished and successful. But the war had left its imprint on the generation of bookbuyers that survived. Their restlessness drove them away from scholarship and their cynicism did not make contemplation or thoughtful literature attractive to them. It was a generation that was trying to lose its disillusionment in pleasure. So publishers had to work twice as hard for half as much success as they had enjoyed in the old days. Harry Batsford had to navigate the ship through some storms of disappointment in the years that followed.

His quarter-century tenure as managing director of his firm has been in circumstances which might have defeated a lesser man. The ephemeral boom after the Armistice of 1918 soon subsided, to be followed by a period of plodding endeavour during which, under his wise leadership, the business flourished in spite of high prices, increased competition and the apathy of post-war society. It was Harry Batsford's energy alone which produced the fine series of books during the years between the end of the war and 1924, when Charles Fry

H*

joined him. Fry has written a note on this time, in which he says:

"I slowly learned the value of my chief. During the years before I joined the firm he shouldered the entire editorial work. I used to talk to our authors and I learned from them what his help had meant, with his encyclopædic knowledge of our subjects. I think that his enthusiasm carried him through; his enthusiasm for all that was best in art, architecture and design, his friendly assistance, and the vitality and gay, playful humour with which he overcame dark moments.

"When I first entered the firm I knew little or nothing about architecture, craftsmanship or the heritage of the English countryside. I wasn't really interested, for my tastes then ran in more strictly literary channels. But before I had worked at Batsfords for a week 'Mr. Harry' had communicated to me something of his own insatiable enthusiasm. As this grew I began to make use of my unique opportunity to profit by his knowledge. He was never miserly over what he knew, as some scholars can be. He liked to share and he liked to see others catch fire from his own energies and enthusiasms.

"His knowledge was, and is, as astonishing as his memory, at which I have never ceased to wonder. It embraces all the by-lines such as astronomy, physics, theology, natural history, geology, and even railway locomotives. He was, and is, an individualist in the best sense of the word, hating fiercely any regimentation or bureaucratic interference. With this independence, which means that he will draw his sword ruthlessly against an adversary, goes a fine sympathy and championship of all suffering or weak creatures. He loves, for instance, the smaller animal and insect life. I can remember, in the old Holborn days, the shocked surprise of a rather superior woman secretary who was sent off to the gardens at Lincoln's Inn Fields with a tiny caterpillar which 'Mr. Harry' had found on the pavement outside the shop.

"He has always been adored by his staff although, heaven knows, he can have bursts of impatience. Then come volleys of lively invective, which relieve his feelings and do not hurt the staff's. He drives his staff hard, yet they enjoy the atmosphere which he creates about him. I have seldom seen him sitting still, and chain-smoking ten to the dozen, he will jump up and down during a conversation, darting about the room in time with his ideas. The jobs of his secretaries have never been sinecures, but they never know a dull moment.

"There is another side to the picture. It has always seemed to me that Harry Batsford draws much of his strength from his immense love of the country. It is curious that so innately restless a person should be a worshipper of long tranquil distances. In our frequent tours of the country together, a story which will be told in its place, I have always noticed that he will go to any labour, whether travelling on foot, by bicycle or by car, to reach the exact viewpoint, carefully worked out before from an inch Ordnance map, from which his enthusiasm will be best rewarded. Hector Bolitho has written of the delight it is to talk of London to him. I have known the equal pleasure of wandering over the countryside with him. No one, I think, knows and loves England better than he. Except for annual holidays, usually spent in scouring the less-known parts of Europe, nearly all his scanty leisure has been used in exploring the English countryside, in the earlier days by bicycle and in later days by car. To me, these trips with him have always been a revelation. One does not know what one has missed, even of a familiar district, until one has explored it in his company."

XIII

By the end of the 1920's Harry Batsford, Hanneford-Smith and Charles Fry realized that their business had outgrown the old house in Holborn. After thirty-five years, with the accumulation of books and papers, there was barely room to move. Indeed it was an unexplained miracle how the building failed to collapse under the weight piled within it. All this happened as the character of Bloomsbury was changing. Business men were invading the quiet old squares. The brass plates of big firms were being screwed on the doors of houses where generations of London families had grown up and died. The householders of Bloomsbury migrated west, and Batsfords followed them, to No. 15 North Audley Street, where they have published and sold their books ever since.

As I have said, Napoleon's gibe against the English was

more or less a compliment, if we consider London shops as they were before the birth of the big store and the growth of monopoly. One of the adventures I first found in London, when I arrived a quarter of a century ago, was among those small, essentially personal shops in which the placid and secure shopkeepers, eschewing advertisement and flamboyance, served their customers in an atmosphere of tradition and modesty. Buying a hat from Lock, an umbrella from Brigg, riding breeches from Tautz or a pair of shoes from Lobb were not sharp business transactions in which one had to watch one's bargain with shrewd care. One knew that craftsmen worked somewhere behind the old fittings, and that with these men the word service was not looked upon as a synonym of subservience—not by those old gentlemen who guarded their good name with the same care with which a parson might preserve his parish registers.

It cannot be hoped that this noble aspect of old London life will survive very long. But let us enjoy it while it stays. Yet one imagines that good craftsmanship will always find its patrons, even in a world where thought itself is mass produced. And one hopes that there will survive just enough individualists to kick against the thrust of progress and insist upon wearing shoes that have not been made of some synthetic stuff; who will appreciate the modest poetry of a handmade watch and the pleasure of opening a book which has been sewn by hand and printed by a craftsman who appreciates the proportions of a well-set title-page and the relation between a page of print and its margin.

Batsfords have clung to that tradition. They are the last of the eighteenth-century company of publisher-booksellers, to whose shop you may go on the day when a book is published and know that the volume you are buying was produced in the rooms upstairs; that it was carried through the same door as you entered, by its author, and that printers and binders all came by the same way, to make it into a book.

No. 15 North Audley Street is still a house, in spite of the great stocks of old books that fill its rooms. There are ranks of wine bins in the cellars and a pleasant 1790 grate in one of the rooms on the top floor. It was very much in the tradition when Professor Richardson was called in to design the appropriate Regency shop fittings, and the shop front, which all fit into the mellow picture.

22. The Premises at 15 North Audley Street, Mayfair.

23, 24. The Shop-front at
15 North Audley Street.

So Batsfords were established in Mayfair, where we know them to-day. There was a gallery on the first floor of the new house, which suggested one more string to the firm's bow; it must have exhibitions. So there was an exhibition of the work of Paul Nash and of the designs of that great innovator C. F. A. Voysey; a show of Cecil Beaton's photographs and of the modern embroidery of Rebecca Crompton. When the French Exhibition was held at Burlington House Harry Batsford went off to Paris and collected a unique show of historic French masters, to be exhibited in the gallery as a complement to the bigger display at the Academy.

We come to the story as we know it to-day. For authors, Batsfords weave a special web of charm. I have said somewhere else that writers like to argue with their publishers. But there is more in it than that. A writer is a lonely sort of creature. Unless he is a vain fool, he always takes his public success with a pinch of salt. He may become quite a person in his way, with honours and the comforts that money brings. But these do not remove the loneliness of the craftsman who cares about his work; about the shape of a sentence and the clarity of an idea. Of course, there are those illustrious ones who soar into the dazzle of being best-sellers, with a world of devoted old ladies to butter them up, and every sign of security from want. But they are the few. There are those who work on quietly from year to year, grateful if they have enough to buy a bottle of wine with their dinner and a good drawing or two for their walls; who like money for what it buys and not for itself; who write books because they love the whole trade of book production; who wish to know their printer and to thank their bookbinder for his part in producing their book; who look upon the whole art of book production as one in which writer, publisher, printer, binder and bookseller are linked together by something stronger than contracts and estimates.

It is not sentimental nonsense to feel in this way about one's books. It is not an affectation for a writer to squirm when he sees somebody place a glass on a volume, or turn down the corners of its pages. Few objects call for the co-operation of so many craftsmen as a book. And when the author finally calls on his publisher for the six copies which are his due (for I despise the dullard who could wait another day for them to arrive by post) there is a great satisfaction in taking one of them in his hands, looking first at the spine, where his name is printed, then testing the binding, and then folding back the dust sheet to see the boards and the colour of the linen . . . sliding his palm along the spine and the edges and realizing that however modest the talent he has been able to give, however small the place the book may take in the great tide of books, it is his own work . . . his labour, just as a fine brick wall is the labour of the bricklayer, or a smooth-running drawer the work of a cabinet-maker.

I do not know whether other writers feel this . . . the anxious but satisfying pleasure of being published. That pleasure is doubled when one is able to deal with a friend like Harry Batsford. Being a quarrelsome and restless creature, I have been to many publishers in my day, for this is the thirty-fourth book which I have written or edited, in twenty years. It is with a deep sense of satisfaction that one finds the publisher who will move heaven and earth to find the binding you wish, the paper you like and the jacket that pleases you; who will take you to lunch with the printer so that you may talk of type and of that delicate and important problem the title-page, upon which author and publisher make their statement.

I am not going to pretend that Batsfords are the only publishers who have made me happy. I recall months of contentment when Sir John Murray published one of my biographies; when I sat for hours with my friend John Grey Murray, going over proofs, accepting suggestions which were made with wisdom and kindness. And I shall always treasure my memory of the years when Cobden Sandersons were my publishers, before they fell into liquidation purely because they cared too much about the quality of their books and too little about their profits. The day may pass when authors are able to enjoy this background to their work; this sense of belonging to a trade which is an affiliation of craftsmen, each equally important in the production and selling of a book. I do not imagine that it is a relationship that will interest people outside our world, but as this is a book for the trade, it is not amiss to point out these things in passing.

25.   The Front Shop at 15 North Audley Street.

26. The Centre Shop at 15 North Audley Street,
with a glimpse of the Back Shop.

XIV

Batsfords moved into North Audley Street in 1930. Other booksellers followed in the migration to the West. Maggs moved from the Strand to Conduit Street and thence to Berkeley Square; Bumpus moved farther west along Oxford Street and Heywood Hill opened his charming little shop in Curzon Street. So a new element came into the life of Mayfair. But Batsfords chose an unfortunate time for their transfer: almost as soon as the fine fittings were finished and the great rooms filled with books the slump of the 'thirties began. It is a part of the story best left to Charles Fry. He has written:

"The existence of a firm like ours depends upon its capacity for renewing itself in each generation. During the decade following the last war Batsford books became less formidable in price than the fine volumes which Bradley and Herbert published in the first part of the century. But they were carefully prepared and richly illustrated, designed for collectors, and were on the subjects in which we had always specialized. The financial depression of the 'thirties brought a crisis which we had to weather, and the only way to do it was to change our fashion to suit the times. A wider public had to be reached with books of a cheaper price.

"Those were anxious times for any publisher, and it was almost entirely through Harry Batsford's steadfastness of purpose and clarity of vision that we finally weathered the storm. For Mr. Harry adds to his other talents a remarkable flair and facility for figures that allows him to make light work of the complex financial organization of the business and the unromantic stuff of auditors and balance sheets.

"But I think the remarkable aspect of the changes we made was Harry Batsford's willingness to listen to the young. His eldest nephew, Brian Cook, had come into the firm; a young man with a unique talent for design and for painting highly coloured book jackets. We met and talked over our plan. We would begin an entirely new kind of book . . . the writing to be on subjects akin to our own . . . Britain, its churches, its houses and its landscape. But we planned to put more than a hundred illustrations in each book, to present them with Brian's attractive wrappers, and in editions so big that we could afford to sell the books for as little as seven shillings and sixpence each. Harry Batsford, steeped in the traditions of a very different kind of publishing, was as adaptable as we were. Brian and I will always remember his unfailing faith in our judgment and his sympathy with our ideas, even when they did not tally with his own.

"This perhaps is symptomatic of one of the most important and attractive facets of Harry Batsford's character. It grows out of his selfless love for the firm and his faith in its survival. In all his business and personal affairs it is the firm that comes first, and has always come first. It is small wonder that it has prospered under his leadership.

"We began our new type of publishing with *The British Heritage Series*, planning to tell thousands of people of the riches of the land in which they lived. Production prices were at a high level. We set out to produce a volume with about 40,000 words of letterpress, with about 130 good photographs, one or more colour plates, numerous line drawings, picture endpapers, and one of Brian Cook's sumptuous jackets in colour. The only economic solution was to take the bull by the horns and print a first edition of 10,000 copies.

"But would the public be interested in books on Cathedrals, Parish Churches, Castles, and Country Houses to that tune? The risk was justified, for we have published about twenty-five of these books and nearly all of them not only sold their ten thousand but have run into further printings, some into fourth and fifth editions. *The British Heritage Series* told the country about its landscape, castles, churches and houses. We followed it up with *The Face of Britain Series*, which treated the scenery and antiquities of the British Isles in a range of volumes devoted to their natural rather than geographical divisions. These were equally successful.

"There was a certain amount of opposition to our success. Elderly architects and some old customers said quite frankly that Batsfords were going to the dogs. Others with vision, and a wish to see the mass of people appreciating the value of England's beauty, applauded our effort; among them Professor Richardson and Mr. Arthur Stratton. Younger architects, of the type that writes critically of the work of others, so industriously that they never have time to do any work themselves, said that we were prostituting architecture and history by making it available to the general public. For years one or two writers have pursued our books with obloquy; especially an unholy alliance of a waspish little writer of funny verses and odds and ends, and an austere, would-be, latter-day Cotman. But the enemies of our project were few. The books sold in thousands, and they continue to sell.

"One of the best tributes to our plan came from James Agate, who wrote:

'Messrs. Batsford, the publishers, ought to be bankrupt, and I will tell the reader why. Every publisher will tell you that he publishes rubbish, and vast quantities of rubbish, because if he didn't he would go bankrupt. Money, they will tell you, is made solely out of rubbish, and it is the enormous sales of rubbish which permit them to publish good books. Now, Messrs. Batsford apparently publish only good books. Ergo, as Shakespeare used to say. But Messrs. Batsford are not bankrupt, have not been, and are not going to be. Yet, as I have said, all their books are good books, and how it is done remains a mystery. . . .'

"There were many appreciations to reassure us. I have a newspaper cutting in which Sir John Squire wrote, 'Messrs. Batsford have the double secret of illustrating their books beautifully and publishing them at prices which are lower than, in times like these, we have any right or reason to expect'. *The Contemporary Review* said that our books 'on British landscape, architecture and customs' were 'almost unrivalled in the world', and after our second series had established itself *Time and Tide* said that 'it has long been accepted that, for a reasonable price, Messrs. Batsford produce the best illustrated books in England'.

"These first favourable opinions have continued with the growth of the series, e.g. in her recent *Country Ways* Esther Meynell has written:

'Having laid the foundations, as it were, with building construction, one may then proceed to enjoy the elevation with some of the enchantingly illustrated books produced by the firm of Batsford, such as the one on *The English Cottage* by Harry Batsford and Charles Fry, *English Village Homes* by Sydney R. Jones, and *The Story of the English House* by Hugh Braun, to speak of only three among all the pause in the narrative to tell the story of the other directors: of Hanneford-Smith, Charles Fry and Brian Cook; particularly must I give a fuller picture of Hanneford-Smith, a remarkable man who always seems to know so much that he reduces me to silence. Since he is the eldest, let him come first. He celebrates his fiftieth year with the firm, just as the firm itself celebrates its centenary. It is a long time for a man to remain faithful to one purpose. Harry Batsford has written of him:

"He came to us in the days before there was strong departmental separation between bookselling, new and secondhand, and publishing, so there is no branch of the business in which he has not laboured. His knowledge of the secondhand books in which we deal is vast, and this is matched by his knowledge of all the technical details of production.

"It was not an easy task for a boy to work for my uncles. But young Hanneford-Smith had character; and he had a background of knowledge. He was the son of Francis Smith, editor of *The Engineer's Year Book* and a kinsman of Sir Francis Pettit Smith, inventor of the screw propeller for steamships. When his father died Hanneford-Smith took over the editorship of *The Engineer's Year Book* which, during the next twenty-one years, grew into a great compendium of over 3,000 pages. It is a book which means little to the layman, but to the engineer it is a bible.

"During all the long last years of Queen Victoria's reign, and through the four reigns that have followed, Hanneford-Smith has never minded the immense amount of detail such work as ours entails. Charles Fry and I are impatient creatures. Hanneford-Smith has been the moderating influence— the patient scholar and the lover of detail—that we needed to balance the team. It has ever been his heart's desire that we should not lose the old line of our publishing, the production of great and fine books regardless of cost. I have always admired the patient devotion with which he has sunk his own separate ambitions to serve the firm. Almost the only way these great books can be published now is through private subsidy. There could never be suitable return for the scholarship Hanneford-Smith has poured into such work. Especially notable works published under his direction are the great monograph on the *Life and Work of Paul de Lamerie*, the Huguenot goldsmith, by the late P. A. S. Phillips; the three-volume

"But my chief interest has been in the production of big books, to which Mr. Harry has made such kindly reference. Following the fashion of our eighteenth-century predecessors, we have usually included in our more important publications

LIST OF SUBSCRIBERS

HIS MAJESTY KING GEORGE V
HIS MAJESTY THE KING OF SWEDEN
HIS ROYAL HIGHNESS THE PRINCE OF WALES. K.G.

His Grace The DUKE OF ARGYLL. K.G., K.T., G.C.M.G. G.C.V.O.

The Right Hon. Sir WILLIAM R. ANSON, Bart., D.C.L., LL.D., M.P., Warden of All Souls' College, Oxford.

Sir WALTER ARMSTRONG, Kt., Hon. R.H.A.

The SOCIETY OF ANTIQUARIES of London.

The ARCHITECTURAL ASSOCIATION, London.

The ARCHITECTURAL BOOK CLUB Zingari, per R. Phené Spiers, Esq., F.S.A. Honorary Secretary.

The PUBLIC LIBRARY OF SOUTH AUSTRALIA, Adelaide.

PETER ADAM, Esq., Kidderminster.

WILLIAM D. ADAMS, Esq., Montreal.

ARTHUR ACLAND ALLEN, Esq., M.A., M.P., L.C.C.

Messrs. E. G. ALLEN AND SON, Ltd., Booksellers, London.

H. W. ANDERSON, Esq., A.R.I.B.A., Adelaide.

JAMES ANDREW, Esq., Glasgow.

ARMY AND NAVY CO-OPERATIVE SOCIETY, LTD., Book Department, London.

The Rev. W. MAURICE ARNOLD, M.A., Univ. Coll. (Oxon), Crowhurst, Surrey.

W. S. ASCOLI, Esq., Manchester.

ALFRED W. ASTON, Esq., J.P., Epsom.

Messrs. ALFRED ATKINS, F.R.I.B.A., AND ROGER BACON, A.R.I.B.A., Wellington, N.Z.

GEORGE W. ATKINSON, Esq., Leeds.

AUSTRALIAN BOOK CO., London.

Her Grace the DUCHESS OF BEDFORD.

The Right Hon. EARL BATHURST, C.M.G., D.L., J.P.

The Right Hon. EARL BEAUCHAMP, K.C.M.G.

The Hon. MARSHALL BROOKS, M.A. (Oxon), J.P.

His Excellency G. BAKHMETEFF.

The BARON DIETRICH VON BOESELAGER.

BATH PUBLIC REFERENCE LIBRARY.

BELFAST MUNICIPAL TECHNICAL INSTITUTE, per F. C. Forth, Esq., Principal.

BIBLIOTHEK DES KGL. KUNSTGEWERBE-MUSEUMS, Berlin.

BIRMINGHAM CENTRAL FREE LIBRARY.

BIRMINGHAM MUNICIPAL SCHOOL OF ART.

BOLTON PUBLIC LIBRARY, per Archibald Sparke, Esq., F.R.S.L., Chief Librarian.

BRIGHTON PUBLIC LIBRARY, per H. D. Roberts, Esq., Director.

BURLINGTON FINE ARTS CLUB, London, per J. Beavan, Esq., Secretary.

Mr. BAIN, Bookseller, London.

J. G. A. BAIRD, Esq., Haddington.

Messrs. HERBERT BAKER, F.R.I.B.A., AND F. K. KENDALL, F.R.I.B.A., Cape Town.

Messrs. J. J. BANKS AND SON, Booksellers, Cheltenham.

GEORGE FORBES BASSETT, Esq., M.A. (Oxon), Southampton.

Mrs. C. E. RIDLEY BAX, London.

A. R. BAYLEY, Esq., B.A., Pembroke College (Oxon), F.R.Hist.S., Malvern.

W. GEDNEY BEATTY, Esq., New York.

CHARLES BEDDINGTON, Esq., London.

JOHN BELCHER, Esq., R.A., F.R.I.B.A., London.

Mrs. HAMILTON BELL, St. Ives, Hunts.

Lieut. H. WILBERFORCE BELL, Pembroke College, Oxford.

Mrs. BERKELEY, Spetchley Park, Worcester. (3 copies.)

Miss A. E. BIBBINGTON, Chapel-en-le-Frith.

Messrs. BICKERS AND SON, Ltd., Booksellers, London.

The Rev. C. R. D. BIGGS, D.D., M.A. (Oxon), SS. Philip and James' Vicarage, Oxford.

CHARLES JAMES BILLSON, Esq., M.A. (Oxon), Winchester.

Mr. B. H. BLACKWELL, Bookseller, Oxford.

J. F. BLAKISTON, Esq., Bankipore.

The Rev. CANON BLUNT, M.A. (Oxon), Newbury.

Monsieur ROBERT BOKER, Hon. Corr. Member R.I.B.A., St. Petersburg.

The Rev. HENRY BOYD, D.D., Principal of Hertford College, Oxford.

The Rev. B. W. BRADFORD, M.A. (Oxon), Broughton Rectory, Banbury.

Messrs. BRENTANO'S, Booksellers, Paris.

HARRY BRIDSON, Esq., M.A., Univ. Coll. (Oxon), Bolton.

WALTER H. BRIERLEY, Esq., F.S.A., F.R.I.B.A., York

The First Page of the Subscription List of Vallance's
Old Colleges of Oxford (1912).

a printed list of the names of the subscribers. This is now almost a dead fashion and it might therefore be explained. These subscriptions were in no sense subsidies. They were secured in response to announcements issued from time to time, intimating our intention to publish such and such a book on English Architecture, Decoration and kindred subjects. They were actual orders placed in advance and were thus a compliment to the reputation we had made. These subscriptions always ran into hundreds and they sometimes reached a thousand; a pleasant tribute to us, since the books were big and expensive.

"Mr. Harry has written of my delight over the actual work of book production. The labours of fifty years have not dimmed that pleasure. But he has not mentioned one book I worked on which must have created a record in publishing. This was in 1924, when Batsfords were commissioned by Ernest R. Graham, head of the famous Chicago firm of architects, to produce under my personal supervision a comprehensive record of his firm's works during the previous forty years. The magnitude of this task can best be shown in the fact that it took over nine years to complete. I think it may be claimed that this was the most sumptuous monograph devoted to the work of an individual firm of architects since the publication of *The Works in Architecture of Robert and James Adam* in 1778-1822."

Thus Hanneford-Smith's contribution ends, with little reference to himself or to the monument of work he has set up during his fifty years of association with Batsfords. I cannot pretend to comprehend the measure of that work, because it embraces subjects of which I know very little. But I can, as a Batsford author, write a few lines of the pleasure it always gives me to climb the stairs and find Mr. Hanneford-Smith in his office. Strange and wonderful things emerge from the chaos of papers on his desk. He still produces books, almost while you are waiting at his side. He brings a certain courtliness into business which makes it possible for him to hand one a cheque as if one were entitled to it . . . a gift few publishers achieve. Perhaps it is the measure of his life that he has travelled from the days of Gladstone and Salisbury to the darker days of Hitler and Mussolini without losing a speck of his integrity or a wisp of his courtliness . . . bringing them both through the hazards of half a century, into a day when they are needed more than ever.

27.   William Hanneford-Smith.

28.   Charles Fry.

XVIII

Charles Fry is the next figure in the Batsford collection. As has already been told, he joined the firm in 1924 as Harry Batsford's personal assistant, and soon became a director. Charles, so far as he knows, has no antecedent connections with the book trade. His father's family were Quakers and his mother's mostly sailors—"Jackie" Fisher was his great-uncle. He himself was destined for the Navy, but left it after his period of training to seek a career elsewhere. He came to Batsfords by a lucky chance, when a job was open. The man who effected the introduction betted someone five bob that Charles wouldn't stand the pace for six weeks. He has stood it now for nearly twenty years.

Let the walls of his office tell the first part of the story. Two of them are a mass of untidy books, on shelves reaching to the ceiling. On the other walls are a drawing by Walt Disney, two watercolours by Rex Whistler, a magnificent architectural drawing by Guardi and two small and exquisite eighteenth-century oils by French masters. The desk is a bewildered muddle of manuscripts and proofs, with just enough space of blotting paper for Charles to doodle upon all the time he is talking. There are two telephones into which he shouts more than he speaks and an ash-tray piled high with cigarette ends.

Charles's praise for an author is guarded, so that the slightest compliment from him is to be treasured. His scorn is like a hive of bees let loose. To watch him planning a book, choosing illustrations and placing them, is a revelation. He is modest over his own efficiency, and the best compliment to his work lies in his loyalty to the name of Batsford: a loyalty so fixed that one simply cannot imagine him in any other setting. Harry Batsford has said of him, "It is impossible to imagine a time when he was not one of the vital, integral parts of the firm". The nineteen years and more of his service with Batsfords have made it all of his life and the full measure of his interests.

Harry Batsford is best able to take up the story from here. He writes: "My mind always compares Charles' deep and abiding attachment to the firm with that of Ulster to the British Crown and Empire. It has recked little of storms, upheavals and low tides of depression, and has shone forth in an ever brighter and stronger loyalty and affection.

"The psychological side," continues Harry Batsford, "is perhaps reflected in his almost unchanged outward appearance and manner since he came to us in 1924. He is still pink and plump, hatless and without a waistcoat. His sardonic humour is ever ready, and if there are on occasions thundering storms, the sun soon breaks through again.

"He has himself written later of our change-over from the rooted traditional methods of publishing to wider fields which, unless blighted by post-war frosts, may well expand still further. His training followed the regular accepted lines of every sort of job, with the result that he is entirely equipped for anything connected with editorial work or production. He can illustrate, tastefully, illuminatingly and effectively, any subject under the sun, and if it can't be pictured by all the photographs and prints on God's earth he will produce an illustrator who will exactly fill the bill. He delights in the intricacies of make-up, of welding text and plates into an attractive and well-balanced entity.

"Charles Fry threw himself heart and soul into the problems and possibilities of the move to North Audley Street, and the fine appropriateness of the new fittings is chiefly due to him. If urban in upbringing, he has found his way to an appreciative understanding of the countryside and its life and work, though he seldom contemplates permanently settling there; and he has acquired of his own volition a considerable critical knowledge of architecture generally and churches and houses in particular.

"Charles can never suffer fools gladly, or at all, and he keeps a devastating broadside to demolish the irritating, the ignorant, the inquisitive and the inane. We are told that the social side is all important for publishers nowadays. In this, Charles, with his ramifying connections, is a solid bulwark. I am a non-gregarious bohemian, addicted to work at home; Hanneford-Smith is the family man *in excelsis*, never missing his regular train to Gravesend. Charles has conjured forth genial friends with helpful contributions of capital; he digs up bright lads, encourages them to write and licks their stuff into presentable shape. If they occasionally turn and rend him, that is only to be expected of human nature, at least in wartime; they always come back to the fold. He is the only member of the firm to cross the Atlantic on business, and he has made five helpful trips to contact colleagues and representatives in the United States. His affectionate fellowship with my nephew Brian Cook is now of fifteen years' standing, and the pair supply the originality of outlook of the younger generation as a foil to the traditional experience of Hanneford-Smith and myself."

XIX

So we come to the last of the four male directors, Brian Cook, whose mother, also a director, is Harry Batsford's sister and a daughter of Henry Batsford, the middle one of "the brothers" who built up the firm's strength in the nineteenth century. Brian is very different from his Uncle Harry and different from Charles Fry. He is less spontaneous in temper, guarded in what he says, inclined to sit back and watch, with a lively eye, the caprices of those less composed than himself. It is in him that the talent of Raphael Angelo Turner, his great-great-grandfather, has flowered again, but in the fashion of his own time. He entered the business in 1928, after being educated at Repton, where he already showed his talent in his paintings and drawings, improved under the instruction of Arthur Norris, the art master, son of the then Dean of Westminster. When he left school Brian had to decide whether he would be an artist and an artist alone, or whether he would take his talents into the firm and adapt them to the needs of publishing. His affection for the firm was as robust and lively as that of his mother, so he became a publisher, with his talents to aid him, and designed and painted in his spare time.

Harry Batsford can best tell the story of his work with the firm. He has written:

"In addition to Brian's art contributions to our books, he has also acquired a thorough knowledge of editorial and production work, and a number of the firm's most arresting

79

publications have been produced under his supervision. He can handle with remarkable ease the most complicated and difficult make-ups—such as appear in the Cecil Beaton books. The contribution of his brightly coloured jackets has accomplished a great deal in giving a distinctive note to the appearance of 'Batsford Books', and has a still growing influence on their popular appeal and on their remarkable sales. This has perhaps been even more marked on the other side of the Atlantic, where Scribners' representatives have said quite frankly that they are the chief factor in their American success. Many are produced by the Jean Berté process, the technique of which Brian has worked out on individual lines for a whole range of effects. The design is schemed for four to five colours, and is then cut on rubber plates and printed in water-colour inks on a fairly rough cartridge paper. If a jacket is reproduced by the ordinary four-colour half-tone process and printed on art paper, it quickly tears and soils, with even a slight amount of wear.

"Brian has thrown himself into many varied activities. He is a political speaker of remarkable and able attraction, and has identified himself very largely with educational movements which have promise of great possibilities after the war. The British Council called upon him to make use of his knowledge and ability in spreading an appreciative understanding of the old country, its appearance, treasures and heritage, in various parts of the world, and sent him on a remarkable trip all over the countries of Northern Europe in one of the coldest Januaries for many years, just before the tide of war swept over the whole of those smaller nations. He has also made two extensive lecture tours in Canada.

"Brian used to take charge of work of a different kind of layout—the setting up and display of the stall at the *Sunday Times Book Exhibition* at Olympia each early autumn. There was great play and much fun with gigantic lettering scrolls, rolls of coloured drapery, show cards, framed pictures, which were combined into an effective and distinctive whole. These exhibitions were equally enjoyable to all who took part in them; the war guillotined the 1939 one, but we look forward to the time when they will come again.

"Brian Cook brings to the firm the lively, fresh outlook on life and business of a young man, coupled with a knowledge of what the firm has managed to carry out in the past. His work in promoting the 'new deal' publications in the last ten years has been referred to by Charles Fry, who has also mentioned some of the highly individual motor tours which they have made with myself. With all this is linked a lively and playful sense of humour which is never more to the fore than when things seem to be taking a wrong turn. He is cheerful— that is his most attractive quality. It showed itself at the age of six when he was caught under my bed, tying horse bells to the mattress, so that when I jumped into bed there would be a cheerful peal.

"For over two years now Brian has been in the R.A.F., but he is able to keep in touch with the firm, and he and his colleagues look forward to the day when he will be once more fully among them.

"There is one more member of the editorial staff who must be mentioned before I hand the story back to Bolitho. Seven years ago Samuel Carr joined us after an education at Oundle and Oxford. It may be said that he almost battered his way into the book trade. Sam's passion for reading is only equalled by his passion for the feel and smell of books: he has a fine library of his own and spends much of his leisure in its perusal and extension. It is typical of his zest that, as rather a highbrow young man down from Oxford, he preferred to endure the drudgery of a spell as junior salesman in a Strand bookshop rather than embark on any other career for which his qualifications and connections fitted him. From the Strand he obtained a job with a firm of cartographers, where he gained some valuable experience of production. He finally landed up with us in 1936, by the simple expedient of writing to offer his services. By a lucky fluke Charles was looking for a personal assistant at the time and, because he liked the tone of his letter, and afterwards the look of him, Sam was taken on.

"Almost from the first day Sam took to the business like a duck to water, and in a few months had made himself indispensable. His work so far has been on the editorial side, in which he excels, but he has also become a dab at production, while his bibliographical flair and taste for drawing and painting have found full scope in the other ramifications of the business. His Irish geniality, humour and tolerance make him popular with everyone he meets at Batsfords, and he has thoroughly assimilated the firm's tradition.

81

"Sam has seen three years' service in the Army at the time of writing, but he will be welcomed back directly he may exchange his rifle for scissors and paste, to help build up the Batsford lists of the future."

XX

So we come into contemporary waters. I cannot help, as I gather the story of the recent years of Batsfords together, considering the picture of Mayfair to-day: the Mayfair which suffers from the aridity of war. There are as many Americans as Britons looking into Batsfords' windows to-day, for the army of our ally has invaded Mayfair, willingly from our point of view, and houses where Gladstone dined and the one in which Disraeli smelled the primroses which came up from Windsor are bombed or given over to troops. Jeeps career along the broad roads that lead into Grosvenor Square and American soldiers, caps atilt, meander past the shop, their swinging walk from the hips so different from the precise, genteel pacing of the average Londoner. Batsfords' window looks out on a strange and changed Mayfair.

I am writing this in June, and one remembers sadly the pleasant stir of activity in North Audley Street on just such a sunny June morning before the war. The last spring books would have been rushed to the press. It is 1935 or 1936. The staff, a little more youthful than to-day, without the shadows of war care upon their faces, would be busy all over the building. The shop would be full of customers, women in summer dresses, American visitors and collectors dipping into the great books of architecture, interior decorators searching for ideas. Upstairs in the production department patient Francis Lucarotti would be sitting, capably wrestling with a "cost", but still bestowing his benevolent smile on the elderly and indefatigable representatives of printers, binders, engravers, paper-makers, all angling for orders, who toiled up the stairs to his room.

Charles Fry knows more of Lucarotti than I do, for I have seldom wandered above the first floor, where the directors sit, into the upper reaches of the house, where the books are produced. Charles has written a note for me on this side of the business. "We have always been rather conservative in our use of the manufacturing trades and have given preference to old friends. So Lucarotti is as much a centre of his part of the business as we are of ours; and he is the keeper of his own part of our tradition, for he has been with us for nearly seventeen years. He sits upstairs, lost in a nightmare of figures, the most patient of all of us, willing to look up and smile at any caller, press a cigarette on him, but not always an order. There is a good deal of fixed decision behind his amiable reception, and we know of one old gentleman, a traveller for a firm, who called on us once a week for forty years without melting anyone's heart.

"But Lucarotti has his company of friends in the trade. Such frequent visitors as Kenneth Nicolson of Jarrolds, whose death we mourned in the first year of the war, Harry Wells, who is making the blocks and reproducing the jacket for this book, Herbert Macro of The Westminster Press, who is printing it, and Douglas Leighton, who is binding it, have seldom gone away empty-handed. There is still something of the spirit of the old bookshop in Holborn, where the uncles used to talk over their plans with the craftsmen they employed. We always like to see old friends like George Brodie and William Haynes, up from Edinburgh, and Mark Clowes of the famous firm that bears his name."

Charles Fry has also given a picture of life on the directors' floor, where he works. "The activity on our floor was no less endless. The problem for us was, and is, to cope with the stream of visitors and work on the books in progress at the same time. Perhaps, as the result of a round robin to scores of photographers for illustrations for a projected book, as many as three thousand photographs would arrive, in twenty batches. These would be spread out and classified, and, from an acre of prints, a hundred or so would be chosen.

"Now we have to do most of the work ourselves, for the younger ones are away with the Services. Donald Shore, who used to scamper up and down the stairs between our offices and Lucarotti's, is a Sub-Lieutenant, R.N.V.R., in minesweepers, and Edwin Willmot, who used to share the scampering with him, and draw enchanting, *sub rosa* caricatures of all of us, met a tragic death on active service, as a sergeant in the Far East. Those were busy days. All over the building the house telephones would be buzzing. In my room the button connecting my telephone with Lucarotti's was always breaking off, through constant and over-emphatic use. There were times when one almost envied the order clerks upstairs, and the counting-house staff, who led a more placid existence under the benign rule of Green.

"Visitors to my room were a varied lot. There were many printers and engravers, of course. There were artists, students and amateur photographers with portfolios under their arms, who had to be seen for fear something good might be missed. There were authors who came in for a solid afternoon's work, for we always have a room to spare for any of our writers who feel that they wish to work near the mill. So we would talk over a cup of tea made by Miss Baker, who has a Maskelyne and Devant talent for producing cream buns and cake, or, if the 'Marlborough Head' was open, we would take our problems to the bar.

"In the summer months Sachy Sitwell sometimes had a house around the corner, and when he was doing a book for us, we would often be his first port of call of a morning. I always enjoyed his visits, his interest in all we were doing and the fireworks of his brilliant, discursive conversation. Cecil Beaton might burst in, elegant, excited, hatless, with more photographs and drawings which somehow had to be crowded into an already crowded book. Cecil has been associated with us in nearly all his books; the reproduction and layout of his splendidly varied work would set a nice problem for any publisher, but the results speak for themselves. He writes very well; some parts of his book on New York, which we published, and recently that on the Near East, move from humour and quick perception into brisk and exciting prose. He draws brilliantly, with wit and invention. And he takes photographs as well as, and perhaps better than, any other craftsman to-day. He ties all these talents together with a humour and mind which seem to stand a step ahead of time. But he has another quality which is hidden from his readers and his public. It is his capacity for work and his ruthless pursuit of perfection. In producing a book for him one deals in fractions of an inch. His sense of what a page of print and illustrations should be is immaculate.

"Another of our younger authors is Peter Quennell, whose angular elegance seems to bear the same imprint of style as his writing, and whose black hat seems to be worn as a symbol of his profession. The time I saw him most seriously ruffled was when it was tipped off his head by a drunk at a country fair. Somewhere earlier in this book Harry Batsford has said that he considers Peter one of the best prose writers in English to-day. As much as anybody, I know the pleasure of opening one of his manuscripts, written in his small, exquisite hand, and finding his story unfold itself in sentences that form themselves into a pattern of faultless prose.

"Then we come to Rex Whistler, whose resemblance to a Du Maurier guardsman was prophetic of his war service: he is now an officer in the Welsh Guards. Rex will sometimes seize a pen, in the midst of an idea, and illustrate it with a series of rapid, nervous little drawings, usually of such beauty that when he goes from the room I put them away and treasure them. It is sad to think of those talented fingers driving a tank.

"Occasionally one had to visit an author in the country. A night away from London was usually welcome after the rush of the office.

"There were frequent drives into Wiltshire to see Cecil Beaton in his beautiful little Caroline house, cupped in a combe under a huge horseshoe of chalk downs. Nearby, one might visit A. G. Street on his downland farm, or one might drive into East Anglia to visit you, my dear Hector, and enjoy the quiet of your delightful timbered house and a hospitality that was profuse and courtly. Those trips would alternate with the directorial tours which have been described elsewhere, though perhaps I can add a few touches to the detail. Whatever the object of the journeys, they were always tremendous fun, but the managing director's insatiability for the pleasures of the countryside often put a decided strain on the endurance of his drivers, and sometimes a firm line had to be taken. Brian Cook and I developed a technique, by which, as evening fell, we kept a mutual lookout for the right sort of pub. We shared almost identical opinions in the matter, and, when the pub came in sight, after exchanging a glance we would drive in firmly, leave the car and begin to swap drinks at the bar. Something of the same technique used to be adopted about lunch-time, too. We became extremely clever at managing Mr. Harry, at least on those occasions.

"Lunch was invariably a picnic meal, partly consisting of food bought at the last town, and partly of tinned stuff. Ever since I can remember, a knife has not been forthcoming and the substitute has been a steel engraver's rule, presented to Mr. Harry by the Monotype Company. After a large meal one naturally feels rather sleepy, and when I was the driver I always went through a bad patch, especially on a hot afternoon, until I had had a cup of tea. There was little respite, and in the evening one was generally pleasantly exhausted by driving. I would like to feel some of that exhaustion to-day.

"Those trips are now only a memory, but I do still occasionally go into the country in search of an author. One such whom I have visited regularly since the war is Edith Olivier, at her dreamlike little house in the great park at Wilton, beside the River Avon. This house is restful and exquisite within and without, and Edith's hospitality has a gentle, unique charm. During the bad raids on London I spent an occasional night at the Daye House, and never before or since have I so completely appreciated the calm of country nights, and the fresh beauty of country sunrises in that most lovely of settings, after the fire and terror of London.

"I think that we may claim that the authors on our list to-day form a good cross-section of the literary and artistic talent of our time. In addition to the writers I have already mentioned, Raymond Mortimer, Ivor Brown, James Laver, Oliver Messell, Richard Wyndham, Edmund Vale, Ralph Dutton and Christopher Hobhouse have enlisted themselves under the Batsford standard for at least one book. Christopher Hobhouse, who joined the Marines on the outbreak of war, had just completed his book on Oxford for us. He was killed by a bomb in a redoubt on the South Coast during the Battle of Britain. His death was a bitter loss to English letters, for his talent was mature and his judgment unusual in so young a man.

"And we have published two books by Hector Bolitho, who is editing this book. I don't suppose I can tell stories for or against him, since this is his book and he has the final word. But there is one story I would like to give, of a day when he went into his publishers' office. Hector likes luxury, and admits that this has occasionally kept him on the edge of poverty. So he sometimes affects the part of poor author. One day he paused to speak to the office boy. Hector's manner can be slightly royal and benevolent. He asked the boy what

29. Brian Cook.

30. Harry Batsford with Joseph Lippincott and Cecil Beaton at Ashcombe.

31. Harry Batsford, Charles Fry and Brian Cook with Miss Frances Pitt at "The Albynes", Bridgnorth.

was his ambition. 'To be a writer, sir,' came the answer. 'Don't do that. Be a publisher! They make money. Writers are a starving race,' answered Hector.

"When the office boy told the story afterwards he added, 'I noticed that when he went out he called a taxi and said "Take me to the Ritz" '.

"Our other authors include James Pope-Hennessy, whose first book, *London Fabric*, was accepted by us before he was twenty-one. He later won the Hawthornden Prize with it while serving as a private soldier in Scotland. And we have an unusual number of country writers on our list of the authority and reputation of H. J. Massingham, A. G. Street, Adrian Bell, Sir William Beach Thomas, Frances Pitt and Doreen Wallace; and illustrators including, in addition to Rex Whistler and Oliver Messel, whom I have mentioned, John and Paul Nash, Randolph Schwabe, who has drawn our frontispiece, Mervyn Peake and Osbert Lancaster.

"Trips to the United States made a pleasant diversion for me in the years before the war. It was agreeable to leave England as the autumn fogs and rains were beginning, and after a few days at sea steam into that lovely zone of American weather, the Indian Summer. New York is always an excitement for me: an excitement made richer by the hospitality of the publishers with whom I had to deal. Americans take it as a compliment when one travels three thousand miles to see them on their own pitch, and their pleasure is expressed in the warmth of their welcome. For me, the only flaw in that hospitality was the American predilection for public speaking. It will be long before I forget my horror at being called upon to review certain aspects of the British book-trade to a luncheon of New York publishers. It will also probably be as long before they will forget the stammering ineptitude of my address.

"Batsfords' oldest friends in New York belong to the house of Scribner, and it was a pleasure each year to discuss future projects and mutual plans with Charles Scribner and Gilman Low, in the pleasant office overlooking Fifth Avenue. Other old friends were the Lippincotts, either in the smart, modern New York office on Park Avenue or at the old house in Philadelphia. There was always much to be done in New York, and it was sometimes a relief to slip south for a few days to friends in Virginia, where in a countryside like a more

XXI

I wish to take the narrative from Harry Batsford and Charles Fry for a few pages, to explain an aspect of their relationship necessary to the next part of the story. Although Harry Batsford knows London well, his heart is in the country. And although Charles is willing to be polite to the valleys and hills, his heart is in London. Upon this they stand divided, for ever.

Indeed, a clever author can manage them quite well upon this separateness of tastes. All he has to do is to say "Malvern".

This must be explained. After Munich, the Batsford directors thought it would be wise to buy a place in the country to which the more valuable books and records could be sent and where the business could be carried on if Batsfords were bombed out of London. So they went in search of a big Victorian house and found one near Malvern Wells, two miles towards Ledbury. Harry Batsford adores it, for its view and its sequestered peace. Charles Fry calls it "that bloody awful lobster-coloured villa", which will bring from Mr. Harry, "It is very comforting and restful to work in a house with so little charm that you don't have to look at it".

So Harry Batsford, with some of the editorial, production and accounts staff, packed themselves into the "hearse", the Ford Utilicon delivery-van, and just before the war they moved into the countryside to do their publishing from there —a little over a hundred years after Bradley Thomas Batsford had come up from the country as a boy. Harry Batsford settled into a scene which he loves, "in a pleasant village suburb, the nicest of all the six Malverns", and Hanneford-Smith and Charles Fry remained in Mayfair. Now they visit one another every few weeks, the one singing the praises of his country setting, describing the quire and central tower of the Priory of Little Malvern, or quoting the vicar, who greeted Batsfords with a paragraph in the Parish Magazine: while Charles remains in London, fire-watching among the books in North Audley Street and pooh-poohing the country branch which, poor thing, has "Walton Villa" for a name.

32. Harry Batsford on holiday at Puerto de Soller, Majorca, 1936.

33, 34. Batsfords in the Country: Walton Villa and Malvern Wells.

When the war began this staff was established in the villa and had already settled down to its work. They found in course of time that Malvern Wells, though little affected in the main, had its contacts with the war, and even with troops from overseas. In a letter Mr. Harry wrote a sketch of this unusual setting for a publisher.

"The war has come to Malvern Wells, but we are still carrying on. A few weeks ago a contingent of Belgian Canadians was quartered here; they were interesting fellows, from Cuba, Bolivia and all over the Americas; one sergeant had been a physics professor at Harvard. So now we have notices on the local weighing machines in English, French and Flemish. We walk along after breakfast to find a detachment at P.T. on the common, or drilling on the road outside: *à gauche*, shouts the sergeant. *Un*, *deux*, reply the men as they swing around.

"Our arrival was not wholly peaceful. First we were suspected of being a party of fifth columnists, then of using the villa as an ammunition dump. But the people of Malvern Wells are accepting us now, and we are proving that books can be published in the country as well as in London. As the war has scattered authors, printers and photographers all over the country, it is just as easy to handle them from the Malvern slopes as from Mayfair."

Then Harry Batsford revealed his heart. He wrote: "The surroundings are an ever changing but ever constant joy. On the one hand are the curving flanks of the great hills, in all their varied aspects, grey and white with hoar frost and topped with mist streamers, fog-shrouded, vivid in summer colouring against a deep blue sky, or with the glowing autumn splendour of a group of great beeches punctuating their stretches of russet bracken. On the other side, as the staff raise their eyes from costs, estimates, or wrestling with proofs, they see the wide, slightly undulating expanse of the Severn-Avon plain, with its wooded knolls leading to the flattened cone of Bredon and lesser outliers, backed by the long, straight line of the Cotswold ridge. The gardens are a rainbow joy and the stone walls in early summer blaze red and white with valerian. Tits and chaffinches will dart around the garden, and a green woodpecker fly across to probe the giant ash opposite. There is both solace and stimulus in glancing around to see the lambs skipping round the ewes, the field-circling trek of the tractor, or to hear the deep whirring hum of the thresher.

"The staff have settled down fairly comfortably, with the sole exception of the packer and storekeeper, whose wife and babies were London bred and didn't mix well with the locals. They went back to London and we arranged for him to stay at a farm. He asked to be escorted down the lane at night as he dreaded the dark and was afraid of falling in the pond. And he thought the country too noisy, because of the animals. One night at the farm was enough for him. He has gone back home, even though it meant the loss of his job.

"On the other hand, Marjorie Bryning, who has nobly renounced her secretarial work to wrestle with, and dispose of, the complexities of massed trade orders, has installed herself in a one-room house on the hillside, with a noble canted window, built, it is thought, about a century ago by a professor recluse as his study.

"The Tate Gallery evacuated staff are established at Upton-on-Severn, and we have shared some exploring excursions with them. They are in an old red-brick Georgian house, glorious compared with the Victorian rawness of Walton Villa.

"We have arranged for one of them, John Russell, to write *Shakespeare's Country* in the *Face of Britain Series*, so I have had some short excursions with him to lonely rectories, to churches of lovely monuments but travestied by nightmare Victorian transmogrification, to remote bucolic hamlets and, on one memorable Sunday, to three pleasant members of the peerage in their Renaissance houses of three contrasting types.

"I induced Charles and Sam to come down for the first week-end and we went over to Llanthony Abbey, and rejoiced in that haven of calm, with its friendly, liberal hospitality, among the winding valleys under the high, grassy, sandstone ridges of the Black Mountains. There in the bar-kitchen, with its shining brass and copper, that was once the undercroft of the prior's lodging, we heard the declaration of war on the wheezy old wireless.

"Afterwards Charles drove us madly through the drizzle of the Penygenffordd Pass, calling 'For God's sake let's get a drink before the pubs close'. I told him to get across the little brook at Hay to the station, where you are in England, but he jerked up irritably at the first hotel. 'Yes, indeed, gentlemen,' said the young landlord, 'we are just in Wales and it is Sunday closing, but it is a sad and a great day, so ask what you like and you shall have it!' "

XXII

Charles Fry has described the first part of the war in London. He wrote:

"After the fall of France a quiet seemed to fall upon North Audley Street, though it became increasingly punctuated by the howl of sirens and the distant thud of guns. During those sunny, unforgettable weeks there were few customers in the shop, and business seemed almost at a standstill—though there were always excitements enough. Once the shop staff joined with a crowd in the street to watch an air-battle thousands of feet above—the planes just visible as tiny dots in a very blue sky, trailing their knotted white swathes of condensation. One would dart out to buy every edition of the newspapers—each, alas, more solemn than the last—or spend one's lunch hour gloomily watching the mechanical excavators ploughing up the open spaces of Hyde Park. One frequent visitor to North Audley Street at that time, however, seemed undisturbed by sirens or guns. It was Sir Reginald Blomfield, up from Rye for the day to see us about the proofs of the book he was writing for us (his last) on his master, Norman Shaw. Dressed in a brown alpaca suit and panama hat, with tortoiseshell pince-nez hanging from a *moiré* ribbon, he looked every inch the Edwardian academician, with his large white moustache and goatee imperial. We all admired his imperturbability, and were encouraged by his cool pre-occupation with his work at a time when few of us could think of anything but the impending ruin of the world around us.

"Then, later, the bombs began to fall in earnest, and we would make our way wearily to work each morning through streets ploughed up by bombs and littered with wreckage and broken glass. Some of the staff lost their homes and possessions, but 15 North Audley Street, though bombs fell all around it, remained unscathed, except for broken windows. Once a time-bomb neatly penetrated the boiler-house of a nearby fellow bookseller and lodged itself beneath the boiler. The street was cordoned off for over a week, and the staff would forgather at the corner of Grosvenor Square each morning to make hurried expeditions to the threatened building, with the permission of the policeman on duty, to extract books and papers necessary for carrying on business. That they did, with a real genius for improvisation, from a basement warehouse for secondhand stock in Mount Street. Letters were answered and production details attended to, but there was general relief when the bomb was at last dismantled and we were able to return to the routine of business in North Audley Street.

"About that time I realized that the war was opening up a fresh field for publishers. The Royal Air Force, the youngest of the Services, was writing history while it was making it. Looking back now, one realizes that the best books which have come out about the war in the air have been written by the pilots themselves. The first of them to make any stir was Paul Richey's *Fighter Pilot*, which we published anonymously. Paul was not an easy author to deal with, because he was too much interested in the immediate moment and what he would do in the war next day to trouble about weaving his recent experiences into prose. But he had written a remarkable manuscript, in the heat of the weeks of battle. It was a frank and startling statement of the fighter pilot's mind.

"The manuscript came into my hands when I met Paul again, whom I had known as a member of my club, after the Battle of France. We became friends during the months that followed, when I had to cajole him from his fighter station near London to come up to work with me on the book. He would meet enemy aircraft in combat during the day and hurry up to London to work on his proofs at night. I came upon the restless spirit of the pilot for the first time and I came also, in him, to realize the selfless gallantry and sense of adventure that impelled those men. He would work for an hour and then demur, 'Let's go to a night club!' So, night after night, a chapter would be taken off to the Nuthouse or some other such smoky joint, and there, with bottles at our elbows and a band blaring into the crowded room, we would correct a few more pages for the printer.

"*Fighter Pilot* was published, and it sold 75,000 copies, as quickly as we could produce them. We could have sold twice as many if it were not for the paper restrictions. *Fighter Pilot* began a new phase of publishing for us. It was what the Americans call a war documentary. It was such a success that we searched for more like it, and found them.

"The next book was *Sub-Lieutenant*, by Ludovic Kennedy. On this book I did a certain amount of work in the wardroom of a docked destroyer. Then came *Wings of War*, in which the Air Ministry was interested: an anthology of prose and verse inspired by flight and battle in the air. Then *Infantry Officer*, another manuscript that smelled of the war when it came to us . . . the story of a young officer who had been in France and who, at the time of our preparing the book, was training as a commando.

"So I had a strange mixture of experiences as a war publisher . . . going sometimes to a fighter station to work with Paul Richey on his book, into the wardroom of a destroyer to prepare *Sub-Lieutenant*, and to a town near a commando training centre to work on *Infantry Officer*.

"In the last year we have published an Air Force book of a rather different sort: Hector Bolitho's *Combat Report*, based on the letters and diaries of a fighter pilot friend. Bolitho set out to trace the story of the development of the pilot's mind and character from before the war and into the fire of battle, rather than the story of battle for its own sake. Very few reviewers failed to pay a tribute to his skill in this, and the book went into a big second edition within a few weeks of publication.

"Another war book which is being born as this record is being written is Cecil Beaton's *Near East*, which fulfils, in prose and photographs, all the promise of judgment, wit and sensibility which his first books gave us."

XXIII

We move into the year of Batsfords' centenary, with which this part of the story comes to an end. It might well close with one more picture of Harry Batsford at work in Malvern, still writing and producing books. In November of 1939 he went off to Llanthony with his mother, to write *How to See the Country* for Batsfords' *Home Front Series.* It may be alarming to be told that he wrote 30,000 words in ten days, but the store of his knowledge is such, and his capacity is so great for pouring it into quick and graphic sentences, that it is not surprising to pick up his manuscript and find that the thorny abbreviations and tangled pages fit together into a well-knit piece of prose.

Harry Batsford wrote from the scene of his work: "If you can resist the temptation to get on top of the world by climbing a 1,700-foot ridge, Llanthony Priory is a fine place to work. There have been terrible downpours of rain, but that helps me to stick to the task; indeed, it is part of the pleasure of being here. I don't mind the draughts in the Priory, but my mother feels them overmuch, so we have plugged some of the gaps in the leaded glass with paper. We have to climb spiral stone stairs to wash our hands, and it is a bit of a test of one's serenity and balance to have to drag up fifty-nine winding steps to the topmost bedroom in the south-west tower.

"I have taken some colour photographs of the noble splendour of the late autumn colours in the valley of the Honddhu, which is a grand and gracious piece of country and the reverse of the epithets 'bleak' and 'sombre' which some misguided guide-book writers give it.

"At Malvern, when their work is finished, the staff sometimes walk over the hill ridges to the west. On November 15th, the last day of autumn, we began at Stoke Edith station and then went up over Tarrington Common to the outer rim of that horseshoe welter of the Woolhope Hills, at the mention of whose tangle of limestones geologists scream with delight. It was a perfect, frosty day, of bright, still sunlight. There were clear views over the great sweep of ruddy autumn-tinted vale countryside, from Hereford to the distant Malverns, and south to May Hill.

"Our life here now has as much pattern as that of the rest of the staff in London. Authors, printers, engravers and photographers come down, so I don't lack chances of stimulating business talks. Our own reference library is growing; also we have the help of the resources of the Malvern Library, under Mr. J. W. Lucas, and of Mr. H. M. Cashmore, of the Birmingham Public Library. They seem to like being troubled.

"We have given over one big room to illustration material, and the staff occasionally work late at night, classifying the thousands of photographs. Sometimes one of the girls knocks up a simple picnic supper, and we eat and work and talk. It is a good life, if it were not for the war beyond the horizon."

Then Mr. Harry added this note for me, to close the story:

"It is perhaps apparent to anyone with the patience to read thus far that we have found the Midlands anything but 'sodden and unkind'. We are surrounded by a star cluster of friendly and helpful neighbours. They even drive the car for us, as, very shockingly, not one of the staff can take the wheel.

"The neighbours lavish fruit on us from their gardens and orchards. We repay them when our gooseberries and rhubarb are good enough for eating. So we publish and illustrate and work, with the country coming generously right up to our doorstep. I am cheerfully happy here, and feel there is much to be said for publishing and distributing books from the country.

"I have realized much since I have been living here, with our staff quietly happy, and among neighbours whose friendly kindness recalls in some degree that great passage in first Corinthians. Near to us is a widow lady who will ferret out lodgings, provide a charwoman, arrange furniture or pick fruit, apparently for the sheer joy of doing something nice for somebody else. And nothing can exceed the helpfulness of the people at the shops.

"But if the general impression is of calm and ordered peace, we are not remote from the war. Between the old cottages with their flowering gardens, through the half-timbered streets of historic Ledbury, rumbles a remarkable and endless assortment of war traffic—strange monsters, gargantuan juggernauts such as the ancient highway has never carried before. The fields bear their crops according to the season's bidding, yet there are many varied forms of wartime activity all around, of which it is not possible to write—signs of the intense ramifications of the country's effort. Even the wide fields themselves have been diverted from their usual course, and with ever more ploughing the landscapes wear a greater range of subtly diversified hues as arable replaces pastureland.

"Here the character and mode of life of the folk are

97

essentially and deep-rootedly English, and more than ever one is enabled to realize that there is a distinctly indigenous form of culture, steadfast and abiding, free yet orderly, individual yet not undisciplined. How grievous would be the disaster if this fine and characteristic contribution to civilization were expunged from the face of the land. Let it never be forgotten that its destruction was the supreme aim of the German race. Yet Hitler will be thwarted in this endeavour to violate the English countryside and stamp out its life, which if we are worthy may be preserved for future ages, even if it continues more by the mercy of Providence than by the foresight of any Government.

"I feel that the message our West Country sojourn has firmly impressed upon us is of the peaceful, deep-seated continuity of English life, manifested in the land itself, the habitations set upon it, and the spirit of its people. Yet we realize, with thankfulness for the prospect of victory and of the future to follow, that it is allied to a readiness to accept needful change, and a resourcefulness and determination which have carried the island kingdom through its former struggles, and will enable it to triumph in this, sharpest and bitterest of all.

"But, poor Hector, you are trying to write the story of a firm of publishers, and all I am doing is to write of ourselves as Englishmen. But I honestly find it quite easy to reconcile the one with the other. In fact, I see them as one."

XXIV

Up to now this book has told the story of the development of Batsfords as publishers and booksellers over one century. But the story of this form of book production and bookselling is older than that. When Bradley Thomas and his sons decided to specialize in the production and selling of architectural and engineering books, they were joining a noble succession. There had already been bookseller-publishers in an unbroken line for one hundred years. Before that even, in the reign of James I, the tradition had a beginning.

This succession of architectural publishers, in which Batsfords take their place, can be said to have originated in the early years of the seventeenth century: a history which started in Holborn and flourished there until Batsfords moved to Mayfair. In the rooms behind the present shop, piled to the ceiling, are most of the great books on the subject, and during the strained days of war and in a life which is shorn of beauty, it is pleasant to escape into these lovely rooms and take down book after book, losing oneself in the great past of human achievements in building and art.

The first book on the subject, published in the reign of James I, was Serlio's *Book of Architecture* (1611): a fine piece of early printing and publishing, issued by Robert Peake in a fashion worthy of the reign of a poet (the title-page is illustrated overleaf). Robert Peake was the son of the court painter to James I. He had a printseller's shop by the present site of Holborn Viaduct, actually in Snow Hill, "next to the Sunne Tavern". This must have been at the top of the City side of Holborn Hill and hard by St. Sepulchre's Church, where he was to be buried after an adventurous life. He must have been established there for about thirty years, for he fathered the works of William Faithorne, the well-known engraver, whose portraits and prints, such as *The Apothecary's Shop* and *The Penitent Murtherer*, were produced well into the reign of Charles I.

There had been other publishers before Peake, although

we cannot trace any architectural books from them. For more than half a century before, books had been issued in Holborn. There was the 1550 edition of *Piers Plowman*, "first imprinted by Robert Crowley, dwellyng in Ely-Rents in Holbourne",

The Title-page of Serlio's *Architecture*. Published by
Robert Peake in Holborn, 1611.

and there were publishers at the Saracen's Head, near to the Conduit. In 1558 Roger Warde was in business "near Holbourne Conduit at the Sign of the Talbot", and in 1584 Richard Jones was established at the sign of the Rose and Crown. By Peake's time there were a number who followed his trade.

Holborn became the natural home of books, both new and old. It grew to be the centre of the secondhand bookselling trade, and in time, as in the case of Batsfords themselves, some of these booksellers became publishers, as if by nature.

But the honour of beginning the trade of English architectural publishing probably belongs to Peake. There is a blank of over a century before we come upon another publisher of architectural books: Piers and Henry Webley, in that favourite spot, "in High Holborn, near Chancery Lane", where there was to be an establishment for 175 years.

But let us remain with Peake's story for a moment, for he was a remarkable man. It is curious that the first publisher in this branch of the trade was also a soldier. Peake must have gone on producing prints and selling them, and a book or two now and then, until the Civil War broke out. He did not follow the majority of London citizens who raised their arms as supporters of Parliament, but abandoned his shop, his prints and books, and attached himself wholeheartedly to the cause of the King. And his artist, whose prints he had produced, went with him. Faithorne, with Inigo Jones, Wenceslaus Hollar and Peake, was at the siege of Basing House, where the latter acted as lieutenant-governor.

Peake was afterwards imprisoned and exiled. When the Restoration brought both grace and corruption back to their old dominance in English life, Peake continued as a soldier, no doubt having forsaken his prints and his books. He had been knighted at Oxford by the King, and when Charles II came home Peake became President of the Honourable Artillery Company. He died in 1667 and was buried at St. Sepulchre's Church.

Holborn kept its character for bookselling throughout the Restoration and moved to its noble position of the eighteenth and nineteenth centuries, when so many of the famous bookseller-publishers were established. Round Gray's Inn were John Scott, Charles Davis and the curious, thickset, rough diamond Tom Osborne, knocked

A Holborn Bookshop in the 'Nineties, showing the outside Bargain Stalls.

Another Bookshop of the 'Nineties: James Westell's, of 114 New Oxford Street.

down by Dr. Johnson with a folio and satirized in *The Dunciad*, who reconciled ignorance with astuteness. He went in for huge deals, including the famous Harleian Collection. There was also the great Jacob Tonson.

Several interesting firms who issued catalogues were established in Middle Row, the island group of houses hard by Staple Inn, until it was obliterated in 1867. On Holborn Hill were John Anderson and, for two generations, the firm of William Darton, of the family of the Quaker publishing house to whose latest representative literary fame and death came so soon together. The Darton bookshop, illustrated in a plate in *The Bookhunter in London* (1895), engraved by Darton's own hand, was an elegant Regency design. Like so much more of its age, it was swept away when the Viaduct was built.

There were bookshops galore in Bloomsbury—in Southampton Row, off Red Lion Square, in Great Russell Street, several in Hyde Street, and in the vanished Bozier's Court. Some of these booksellers were curious and eccentric characters; and some of them were among the first to issue book catalogues. Booksellers, secondhand and new, publishers and printsellers are far from absent from the neighbourhood today, particularly round the British Museum. But one hundred to two hundred years ago it must have been a sort of crowded Milky Way of literature, with shops in every little alley. The two Turnstiles leading into Lincoln's Inn Fields were favourite spots; George Hatton in 1636 published his books from "the Sign of the Sun, within the Turning Stile in Holborne".

Of most interest in this connection is that 94 High Holborn was a bookshop half a century before the Batsfords moved into it. There and then John Petheram issued catalogues, of which a few are in the British Museum, entitled *The Bibliographical*

Miscellany, with, as an eight-page supplement, the reprint of a rare tract.

In the century and a half from 1611 publishing gradually became a distinct craft. Its pioneer votaries in the early and middle years of the eighteenth century were not lacking in enterprise; they produced large folio volumes of engraved plates, such as Kent's *Works of Inigo Jones*, James Gibbs' *Book of Architecture*, and Campbell's *Vitruvius Britannicus*, three volumes, with a two-volume supplement by Woolfe and Gandon—which, to anticipate, was later followed by a *New Vitruvius Britannicus* by George Richardson, two volumes, and a further volume some fifty years after by George Robinson.

The war makes it impossible to carry through the research which would probably yield more about the course of eighteenth-century architectural publishing in High Holborn. But the main lines appear fairly clearly, as may be seen by the succession of imprints on the rather few books at present readily accessible.

The first mention of an eighteenth-century Holborn imprint is of H. Piers in 1745, when he was one of half a dozen distributors of Chippendale's *Cabinetmakers' Director*, the first edition. A different set of names appears for the third. But the imprints are headed by a note that the book may be obtained from the author's address in St. Martin's Lane. The form is of common occurrence about that time; it rather looks as if the author, architect, or furniture designer got his book printed, sold it himself, and also entrusted its distribution to a number of bookseller-publishers. Piers was later joined by Webley. One imprint describes them as Piers and Partner and Henry Webley, but the standard form is Piers and Henry Webley. Another list is headed A. Webley. Were they, perhaps, brothers?

Next Henry Webley appears *solus*, and his list is headed "To the Nobility and Gentry, and to every Individual concerned in Building; but particularly to all Architects, Surveyors, Carpenters, Joyners, Bricklayers, Masons, Plaisterers, Stucco-workers, Paper Machée-makers, Ornament Modellers, Cabinet and Chair-makers, Upholsterers, Coach-makers, Painters, Plumbers, Stove-grate-makers, Smiths, &c." from "his original shop for Books of Architecture, Perspective, etc. in Holborn, near Chancery Lane".

Henry Webley issued the fine original folio edition of

Chambers' *Civil Architecture*, 1759, and interesting works by Crunden, and always his place is "nearly opposite Chancery Lane". A work by Crunden, the *Original Designs*, issued in 1785, a quarter of a century later, bears Isaac Taylor's imprint; it seems a legitimate inference that Isaac Taylor the First acquired and carried on Webley's business, as their names never appear together.

A
CATALOGUE
OF
MODERN BOOKS
ON
ARCHITECTURE,
THEORETICAL PRACTICAL, AND ORNAMENTAL;
VIZ.
BOOKS OF PLANS AND ELEVATIONS FOR COTTAGES, FARM-HOUSES, MANSIONS, &c.
TEMPLES, BRIDGES, &c.
OF ORNAMENTS FOR INTERNAL DECORATIONS, FOLIAGE FOR CARVERS, &c.
ON PERSPECTIVE.
BOOKS OF USE FOR CARPENTERS, BRICKLAYERS, AND WORKMEN IN GENERAL, &c.

WHICH, WITH THE BEST ANCIENT AUTHORS, ARE CONSTANTLY ON SALE AT

TAYLOR's
ARCHITECTURAL LIBRARY, No. 59, HIGH HOLBORN, LONDON:

WHERE MAY BE HAD

THE WORKS OF THE MOST CELEBRATED FRENCH ARCHITECTS AND ENGINEERS.

The Title-page of a Taylor Catalogue of *circa* 1790.

It is about 1772 that the imprint of Taylor first appears. The Taylors were an exceptional, talented family, East Anglian and Nonconformist; of their members records exist from 1730 to 1865. Nothing like justice can be done to them here, but an account of the family has recently been published by Heffers of Cambridge, under the title, *The Taylors of Ongar*, written by Doris Mary Armitage, a great-grand niece of Anne Taylor, who married a clergyman named Gilbert. They were connected with Ongar in Essex and the little Suffolk weaving town of Lavenham, still full of delightful half-timbered buildings. Indeed, in 1796 the middle Isaac Taylor published a book of *Ornaments from Lavenham Church*. He was the father of Anne Taylor, and of Jane who wrote the immortal verses, "Twinkle, twinkle, little star".

There were three Isaac Taylors, all engravers, the second also a dissenting pastor, the third a lay theologian. It was the eldest Isaac (1730-1807) who was the first to be connected with the architectural publishing business. About 1752 he made his way to London from Worcester, paying 2s. 6d. for the privilege of walking beside a stage wagon.

An early imprint runs, "Sold by I Taylor at the Bible and Crown in Holborn, near Chancery Lane, 1772". Their place of business was also described as nearly opposite Great Turnstile, but they later called themselves "The Architectural Library", first at 56 and then at 59 High Holborn. An early one-page list describes "Books printed for and sold by I Taylor". It consists of eighteen numbered items, including some by Wallis, Hoppus of "Measurer" fame, and the prolific Batty Langley. Isaac must have been joined by his son Josiah somewhere in the late 1780's, and they worked together for something less than a decade of prolific production. Josiah carried on the business after his father's retirement. A comprehensive six-page catalogue of *circa* 1810, reproduced overleaf, speaks of "J Taylor's Architectural Library, 59, High Holborn".

Isaac Taylor was a Fellow of and Secretary to the Incorporated Society of Artists. There is practically no mention of the book side of his activities in *The Dictionary of National Biography* article or in the recent book on the family, which merely states that he was engaged in a business of this type. The book is largely devoted to the career of Isaac Taylor the Second, of Ongar, his wife and his family, and particularly to the gifted Anne and Jane and their works. The picture of family life it presents is delightful and idyllic.

It is not altogether easy to distinguish the books which the Taylors published from those which they merely sold. But we know that they issued Hepplewhite's *Cabinetmakers' and Upholsterers' Guide* and several works by Sir John Soane, also many *Carpenters' Guides*, and *Practical Builders* by such writers as the fertile William Pain. Quite a number of pleasant little quartos and octavos of good style designs for Rustic Furniture, Shop Fronts, Garden Temples, even Coaches, were issued anonymously, at very cheap rates; they were in all probability initiated by, and engraved for, the Taylors, and testify to their enterprise.

The first separate Josiah Taylor imprint now traceable is

on Pain's *Practical Builder*, 1799, so that it was between 1793
and 1799 that Isaac must have retired and left the business in
his son's hands. He did not die until 1807, some 10-12 years

A

CATALOGUE

OF

MODERN BOOKS

ON

ARCHITECTURE,

Theoretical, Practical, and Ornamental;

VIZ.

BOOKS OF PLANS AND ELEVATIONS
FOR COTTAGES, FARM-HOUSES, MANSIONS, &c.
TEMPLES, BRIDGES, &c.

Of Ornaments for internal Decorations, Foliage for Carvers, &c.

ON PERSPECTIVE.

Books of Use for Carpenters, Bricklayers, and
WORKMEN IN GENERAL, &c. &c.

Which, with the best ANCIENT AUTHORS are constantly
on SALE at

J. TAYLOR's

ARCHITECTURAL LIBRARY,

No. 59,

HIGH HOLBORN, LONDON.

———

WHERE MAY BE HAD,
The WORKS of the most celebrated
FRENCH ARCHITECTS and ENGINEERS.

The Title-page of a Taylor Catalogue of *circa* 1810.

later; his work as the Secretary of the Incorporated Society of
Artists, which paralleled the Royal Academy, was doubtless a
full-time affair, and we can picture the fellowship at his house,
where among others Goldsmith, Bartolozzi and Smirke used

to forgather. He was buried as "Isaac Taylor, gentleman", in Edmonton churchyard.

Josiah continued to publish a number of important works, such as Richardson's *New Vitruvius Britannicus*, 1802, and the fine Repton's *Landscape Gardening*, 1803-5, with its many coloured plates with cut-out flaps of alternative views. His very comprehensive six - page list, dated about 1809, has many items, largely the same and set from the same wording as in the days when father and son were associated. The last imprint of Josiah Taylor which can now be found is dated 1811; it is not known when he died.

Martin Taylor, son of Isaac Taylor the Second, had been apprenticed to a book firm in Paternoster Row, which has now vanished. He succeeded his

BIBLIOTHECA ARCHITECTONICA.

A

CATALOGUE

OF

BOOKS

ON

THE FINE ARTS,

ARRANGED IN TWELVE CLASSES,

AS

A MANUAL

FOR THE USE OF

THE ARCHITECT, ENGINEER, STUDENT, AND AMATEUR;

IN WHICH ARE INCLUDED

WORKS ON THE THEORY AND PRACTICE

OF

Painting and Sculpture,

IN THE POSSESSION OF

PRIESTLEY AND WEALE,

HIGH-STREET, BLOOMSBURY.

A COPIOUS INDEX IS SUBJOINED.

MDCCCXXV.

The Title-page of Priestley & Weale's Catalogue of 1825.

uncle Josiah, possibly after working for him for a time, though this is not mentioned in the book on the family. He moved from High Holborn to 1 Wellington Street, Strand, and published Papworth's quarto edition of Chambers' *Civil Architecture*, for many years current as a reference book. An undated sixteen-page list of *circa* 1830 contains a good varied collection of titles, including the remainder of Britton's *Cathedrals*, but is largely concerned with Civil Engineering. Nevertheless he seems by this time to have been operating on a reduced scale; perhaps the business was declining. It is possible that after nearly half a century of active prosperity he may have inherited sufficient means from his grandfather and uncle to make it unnecessary for him to carry on the firm with the same strenuous activity.

About 1825, in Holborn, we hear of Priestley and Weale, who had published the third volume of R. and J. Adam's great *Works in Architecture*, and a pocket edition of Stuart and Revett's *Antiquities of Athens*. A copy of their catalogue for 1825 is in the Batsford archives; it contains 200 pages, comprising 1,500 items. Priestley disappeared, but John Weale, established at Taylor's old address, continued in business for about another thirty-five years. He turned his attention largely and increasingly to engineering, but published Cockerell's fine folio on *The Temples at Aegina and Bassae*, and Weale's *Quarterly Papers on Architecture*. One of his lists, titled and dated "Architectural Library June 1839", includes a new edition of Pugin's *Public Buildings of London*, Habershon's *Half-timbered Houses in England*, and Tredgold's *Carpentry* by Barlow. As an example of continuity it is noteworthy that in *The Publishers' Circular* of August 15th, 1890, an advertisement of Weale's *Educational Series* lists 116 items, out of 350 then still current, apart from the engineering series, twenty-eight years after his death. The transition from Weale to Batsford is sketched in an earlier section.

XXV

I will leave it to Harry Batsford to show how his firm graduated in the tradition I have just sketched. He writes:

"The record of the Taylors shows what was accomplished by thought and enterprise in eighteenth-century publishing. Batsfords began their career a century later than the Taylors and with fewer advantages. The early lists were a funny mixture, and show how my uncles were struggling, through experiment and error, to form some character for the firm. These lists included quartos of architectural sketches, records of tours, books of contemporary designs for cottages, furniture and so on. There were also practical text-books, and works like *Christian Gravestones* and *Designs for Window Draperies*, which went on selling for years.

"By 1880 the firm had begun to discover its own shape: its own especial character. It had initiated the reproduction of a selection from Robert and James Adam's *Works* which continued for forty years. For all their queerness these early Batsford books are worth looking at; they have something elemental in their archaic primitiveness, but they were definite beginnings.

"Next came the big books of photographs and drawn plates; then the preparation of informative and attractive text-books, a line developed by Herbert Batsford into a co-ordinated series. Nowadays the projects are planned after a close-knit, thought-out pattern, covering a whole group of allied subjects—districts, old buildings, technical crafts, etc. —and these may be added to and enlarged according to the shifting taste of the public. For instance, Renaissance building in England may be reviewed systematically, with all its phases analytically covered and illumined with many comparative pictures.

"A publisher who knows his work is always studying, selecting and discarding; his record is one of ceaseless experiment in pleasing the public, and thus keeping his list healthy; not cluttering it up with books which do not prove themselves. In short, he must learn to marry his own taste to the public desire. He cannot wait for books to be written and brought to him; he must be as enterprising in finding subjects and titles as he is in finding a public. Above all, he must know what to reject uncompromisingly, for most of what comes his way can never see the light. So we may follow how the firm worked its way from tentative beginnings into its own province as publishers of illustrated books: a province reached only after several decades of experiment.

"The sales of these early books were slow, and for a long time the uncles sold most of them direct to customers, at full retail figures: their appeal to ordinary retail booksellers was limited. Now of course our books are sold through retail book-trade channels all over the world. Such sales at reasonable prices are possible because we are usually willing to make a plunge with a big printing order.

"The first four-page list of Batsford publications is dated about 1878, and consists largely of quarto and folio books of drawings, such as Talbert on *Modern Gothic Furniture*, designs of which are, by a curious turn of the wheel, being to some extent reproduced to-day. The veteran Robert William Billings, author of a four-volume book on Scottish buildings, of which the original drawings are in the R.I.B.A. Library, contributed *The Infinity of Geometric Design Exemplified*, an attempt to explore the possibilities of Gothic tracery.

"There were Colling's *Examples of English Mediæval Foliage*, which is still found useful for reference, and the same author's *Art Foliage*. Also included were Fletcher's *Light and Air* and *Model Houses for the Industrial Classes*. Then we find Norman Shaw's *Sketches for Cottages* and Godwin, once Ellen Terry's husband, on *Art Furniture*. Another book, mentioned later (page 112), was Talbot Bury's *Remains of Ecclesiastical Woodwork*, still appealing and valuable; Aymer Vallance was able to prove from one of its plates the extent of the appalling destruction of fine woodwork at Swinbrook, Oxfordshire. In addition to Fletcher's *Quantities*, mentioned earlier in these pages, there were Stevens Hellyer's landmark treatise of *The Plumber and Sanitary Houses*, a pioneer of modern sanitation (the remarkable title-page is reproduced on page 22), and a selection of half-crown books on *Elizabethan Architecture, Town Dwellings, Baths and Washhouses*. Some of the quartos of modern designs published a little later look distinctly curious at the present day—as Dr. C. H. Dresser's *Modern Ornamentation* and Cotton's *Suggestions in Architectural Design*, of which one critic said that the author-designer appeared to be afflicted by the horseshoe arch in its most malignant form.

"The books of sketches and drawings continued to appear fairly successfully for the rest of the nineteenth century, e.g. Maurice B. Adams produced a book of drawings of old English houses, an earlier collection of *Artists' Homes* and later a work on *Modern Cottage Architecture;* R. Phené Spiers contributed some lithographic reproductions of his water-colours of Egypt; and there were a book of sketches by W. Bassett Smith, *Examples of Old Furniture* by A. E. Chancellor, and, by G. A. T. Middleton, *Ornamental Details of the Italian Renaissance*, a poor successor to the efforts of Oakeshott and Kinross.

"All these belong absolutely to a past age. It was well into the twentieth century before the uncles could persuade architects that the day for publishing volumes of their sketches and measured drawings was past.

"Taste changes diametrically. In 1902 Henry Tanner, who is still happily with us, produced an excellent series of measured drawings of *English Interior Woodwork*, which was reprinted. This book is still valuable for reference, but its publication now, forty years afterwards, is unthinkable, so greatly have outlook and methods veered from any collection of the kind. The earliest books of sketches were brought out before 1880—for instance, Bernard Smith's two volumes on France and Switzerland, and on Italy. But the latest of this line were able records of selected subjects, e.g. Bailey Murphy's *English and Scottish Ironwork* and a post-last-war folio of *English Woodwork* by Beveridge, rather on Tanner lines, much of it very elaborate. It is by no means easy to deal with this type of book at the present day.

"Of designs for modern houses, there was *Bungalows and Country Residences* by R. A. Briggs, a breezy figure, invariably known as Bungalow Briggs, who kept a remarkably fine library and was a keen organist. Surprisingly enough, shortly before the last war, he brought out a collection of drawings in colour of *Pompeian Decoration*, and about the same time appeared a series of coloured studies of historic decoration by J. D. Crace, of the great decorating firm. Henry Tanner also wrote the text and contributed the line drawings to W. Galsworthy Davie's photographs of *Old English Doorways*, a book which was actually reprinted and sold after the last war.

"Batsfords were always fond of books on historic ornament: they were an expression of their interests as a firm. Editions were brought out of German collections of coloured plates, and Meyer's justly celebrated *Handbook of Ornament* was published, the English version being edited by Hugh Stannus, F.R.I.B.A. An English edition was also issued of Speltz's *Historic Styles of Ornament*, sponsored by Spiers.

"The late Richard Glazier's text-book on *Historic Ornament*, with his careful drawings, first appeared in 1899. It is still current, in a much transformed and enlarged form. Glazier, who was headmaster of the Manchester School of Art, also wrote for us *Historic Textile Fabrics*, which has sold slowly. The subject is not as popular as it deserves to be, in spite of the fact that England is the greatest textile manufacturing country in the world, and that the Victoria and Albert Museum has as fine a collection of stuffs as may be seen anywhere. The second master at Manchester under Glazier was Henry Cadness, who published a text-book on *Brushwork and Design* in 1902.

"Some of these books seem absolutely freakish nowadays. In addition to a popular work on *Farm Buildings* and one on

Stable Fittings, there were G. H. Bibby's pair of two-shilling booklets on *Workhouses* and *The Housing of Pauper Lunatics*, and a popular book by the late F. A. Fawkes of Chelmsford on *Horticultural Buildings*, which ran into many editions. Fawkes also wrote a tract on *Three Christian Tests*, about the only religious book which the firm has ever issued.

"Tavenor Perry produced two pleasant pamphlets of *Byeway History* on Bletchingley and Plaxtole in the Home Counties. It is unfortunate that there seems to be no scope for little books of this type.

"One of our most interesting links through these early books was with the Gothic Revival. The phase had started to fade in 1882, after the opening of the Law Courts, described by Statham as 'rather a defiant and bewildering memorial of the Gothic fervour of its day'. But fifteen years after, when I joined the firm, Gothic Revival books were still selling, and their influence was still felt.

"Good, solid, standard works, such as James Kellaway Colling's *Details of Gothic Architecture*, two volumes, and *Mediæval Foliage and Coloured Decoration*, and Dollman's *Ancient Domestic Architecture*, two volumes, were not only in steady demand but were actually reprinted from the original stones early in the twentieth century, and with success.

"Talbot Bury's *Ecclesiastical Woodwork*, with copper plates, was reprinted by lithography. T. Talbot Bury was able and versatile, and his fine graphic work deserves to be more appreciatively known and remembered. The original publication dates of these range from about 1865-1875; it is a testimony to their sterling worth that they could be re-issued twenty-five to thirty years later.

"I count it one of the abiding privileges of my youth to have met some of these great figures of Gothic Revival draughtsmanship.

"At the turn of the century Colling was a frail little old bent figure, almost at the end of his resources. Uncle Herbert, in conjunction with J. Osborne Smith, F.R.I.B.A., induced the R.I.B.A. to open a fund for him, and purchase his delightful sketch-books, which show the spontaneous delicacy and firm clearness of his drawing. He was very thankful for and gratified by this mark of recognition, which eased his circumstances until he died a few years later. Francis Dollman, with quite a batch of excellent works to his credit, was a little, rubicund, humorous, lively old man, chuckling reminiscently over the fiery tantrums of old Jobbins, his collaborator. Then there was John Johnson, of *Churches of the Nene Valley*, who, on calling, delivered a lecture on the profiling of Early English mouldings; his collaborator on the book, A. H. Kersey, died only the other day.

"There was a curious recrudescence of the Gothic Revival about 1900, when old John P. Seddon, architect for many years and author of various papers, including one on *The Domestic Gable Forms of Thanet*, came to the Batsfords to publish the record of a remarkable cabinet on which several of the Pre-Raphaelite group had worked—William Morris, Rossetti, who had painted the panels, and others. It illustrated the honeymoon of King René of Anjou, and with much expenditure of time and work a small booklet, little more than a pamphlet, was prepared under the title of *King René's Honeymoon Cabinet*, with collotype plates. It hung about and involved a disproportionate amount of attention, so that Herbert Batsford was wont to say plaintively that he wished King René had never had a honeymoon.

"But if the Gothic Revival has gone and no one weeps its passing, the tradition has remained, and the loving appreciation and close study of medieval art continues with greater insight and more analytical understanding. In the Batsford circle of authors Francis Bond and old Dr. Cox were both, in very different ways, prolific writers on Church architecture and features. Their work is still esteemed to-day, though they passed on at the close of the first world war.

"Another writer whose death in 1934 cut short what would have been a promising career was Frank Howard, of Oxford. He collaborated with Fred Crossley on *English Church Woodwork*. His account of Parish Church style development, published posthumously, was but the introductory sketch to a great study of Local Types in English Churches, which a busy architectural practice never allowed him to finish.

"Aymer Vallance, of whom more is written on page 120, has followed his survey of *Crosses and Lychgates* by an exhaustive account of Screens of Parochial type, the Pulpitums of Greater Churches being reserved for a separate study. Over thirty years have passed since his *Old Colleges of Oxford* was published, and forty-six since his *Art of William Morris*.

"Fred Crossley never stands still in all his activities of designer, restorer, writer, photographer and lecturer. After the *English Church Woodwork* with Howard, he produced a full review of *English Church Monuments*, and more recently has contributed two volumes to the *British Heritage Series—The English Abbey*, a study of its life and work ingeniously dovetailed into a graphic story from original records, and *English Church Craftsmanship:* a sample of that rich inheritance so little appreciated by the British people, who usually tack the myth of foreign origin on to any fine piece of work. Crossley's many papers on his own county of Cheshire are designed to be welded one day into a great and worthy record of its churches and their crafts, a service Munro Cautley has nobly performed for the incomparable fabrics of Suffolk. It is a matter for rejoicing that Crossley has lately finished a review of *English Church Architecture*, for his wide comparative knowledge is allied to a keen critical acumen.

"Charles Fry and I have collaborated in volumes on *English Cathedrals*, now in its fifth edition, and *The Greater English Church.* We dedicated the latter to Dr. G. G. Coulton of Cambridge, whose erudition has found only partial expression in his many studies of medieval life and art, and whose work at St. John's College has trained some remarkable men to spread the knowledge of the Middle Ages he has gathered and made available.

"Only the briefest account is possible of the technical side of the firm's publishing in its sixty-five years' career. The books cover, as might be expected, a wide range of subjects, but there are a number of instances in which one or two moderate editions satisfied the demand, and the book did not require keeping in print indefinitely. The Mitchell pair on *Elementary* and *Advanced Building Construction*, however, celebrate their jubilee this year, and have in half a century sold many more copies than any other single publication on the firm's list. These books have been completely transformed from their rudimentary original state.

"Once at some gathering or other Lawrence Weaver, who was occasionally liable to a touch of the pontifical, solemnly warned Herbert Batsford that he 'had done himself all the harm imaginable by publishing Mitchell's *Building Construction*'. That fired the little man, who said hotly that he only wished he had a score like them, for they were books which would sell merrily long after both of them were years in their graves—a prophecy which has been exactly fulfilled.

"We have already touched on *Quantities;* Colonel Rea's exhaustive analytical survey *How to Estimate* is its junior by a quarter of a century, but is as popular and valuable as ever after a life of over forty years, and parallels equally standard books on Architectural Practice and Sanitation. The series of important works on Practical Building Crafts includes volumes on Masonry, Carpentry, Joinery, Stair-building, Plastering and Cabinetwork, all written by practical men; Brickwork will shortly be added. In addition, manuals have been brought out on Structural Mechanics and Engineering, Handcraft, Architectural and Technical Drawing and Perspective, and Repairs, among a number of other subjects.

"In a trade paper interview with the Batsfords about 1890 it was emphasized that the preparation of the great illustrated books each occupied several years. It might have been even longer when, as occasionally happened, there was a fire at the bookbinders, as at Leighton's in 1904 with Starkie Gardner's *Catalogue of a Loan Silver Plate Exhibition;* the smoke-grimed collotype plates were miraculously salvaged by the cunning of our friend Thomas Leighton. At this fire some books printed on art paper had been wetted and turned into solid slabs, not unlike stable paving blocks.

"The collotype plates of the folio works by Gotch and Belcher were printed abroad, by firms who would nowadays be considered painfully dilatory and unreliable. The text, as it came with costive intermittence from authors, was printed well but expensively by the Chiswick Press at Took's Court, Chancery Lane. When one of the sheets was ready we were asked to go over and pass it on the machine. The office door was always locked, but we were admitted by a huge, raw-boned fellow called Horace. The manager was Charles T. Jacobi, a dapper, alert little man, black-bearded and waxed-moustached, who was a prominent figure in the printing trade, a lecturer and the author of a whole range of books.

"These folios took years to produce, because each photograph had to be specially taken; every drawing specially made. No use was made of pre-existing material, which to-day is found so invaluable, and for Garner and Stratton's *Tudor Architecture* even the Buckler drawings were redrawn. Not until the 1929 second edition were Buckler wash drawings reproduced direct.

"Thus illustration in Edwardian days was by very different methods from those used to-day. Large-scale photographs were taken by special photographers, whom we engaged. Now we send a list to a large number of firms and individuals, and thus cover the face of the land. The position of the photographer of to-day is far higher than it was thirty years ago. In 1910 he was likely to be left with the housekeeper and given the second-best sherry, while the author with whom he was working was ushered into the presence of the family. On one occasion a West Country photographer of considerable substance agreed to drive our author over the country of which he was writing, in his own car. They arrived at a country house, and the author went in to lunch with the family, while the photographer was left to kick his heels at a side door, unfed and fuming. An hour later the author appeared, smoking a fat cigar, and told the unfortunate fellow to crank up and drive away. Apparently the hospitality had gone to his head, for he urged the photographer to hurry as there were so many places still to see. The latter was so furious that he pitched the author's bags on the grass, threw his gloves in his face and drove off, leaving him marooned in a remote corner of rural England.

"Among amateur pioneers in photographic recording mention must be made of W. Galsworthy Davie, an elderly architect, timid but indefatigable, who wandered over South-east England from 1895 to 1910, taking cottages, houses, carving, plasterwork, furniture and metalwork. He was thus a precursor of Brian Clayton (see page 117), who was active two decades later—but Davie was far more restricted in technical equipment and travelling facilities.

"Nowadays photography has become a universally recognized art, and the agencies and individuals supplying illustrations are enterprising and keen. Together and severally the men of the camera are as entitled to bear the motto *Ubique* as the Royal Artillery. They are interested in the books they are illustrating, and are companionable fellows on a journey. I remember with particular pleasure journeys with Will F. Taylor and Herbert Felton, who have enriched many of our books through their enthusiasm and enterprise.

"Some of these later photographers put as much study and devotion into their work as scholarly writers. Brian Clayton first visited our office soon after the last war. He came many times, with masses of delightful photographs which he had taken all over England: church ironwork, carving, houses, bridges, and every form of English craftsmanship. Charles Fry, Brian Cook and I once went to see his collection of nine thousand negatives and thirty thousand prints, in his house by the Wye, at the foot of the Forest of Dean hills, and it was not until then that we discovered that he had been an ace airman in the last war. When he died we bought the collection, upon which we now draw steadily for illustrations.

"We have seen that most of the plates used in the early books were reproduced in collotype, sometimes in Holland or Germany. The worst feature of the process was its infinite variety. This involved sending one of the production staff to examine, say, 2,000 copies of 100 plates and throw out anything too heavy or too pale. Hours of this work were so moidering that it became hard to gauge what was admissible and what called for rejection. By contrast, it was a joy to go up to Edinburgh and pass a running half-tone sheet on a huge machine, and to talk to one of the splendid craftsmen machine-room overseers, such as old Lamont of the Darien Press.

"For years Batsfords had an affection for super-calendered or imitation art paper, which they insisted, if really finely surfaced, could give results little if at all inferior to coated art. Owners of mills who thought that any old half-rolled surface would do for a publisher had a rude awakening, and machine-room heads who reckoned anæmic, underprinted pallor good enough sometimes ended up with the sack after the ensuing skirmish.

"It will have been noted that museum research became a regular part of the firm's work about 1908, and Herbert Batsford made a strong feature of it. There was the Victoria and Albert Museum, staffed entirely by angels, where you never went to the Library or Print Room without some joyous discovery, and the British Museum, in whose Manuscript Department we could enjoy the enormous folios of coloured stained-glass drawings, which used to be trundled along on leather-covered trucks to the bench where we worked. And we could revel in the medieval manuscripts themselves, to choose the pictures of social life we wished to illustrate. Our insatiability must have been a trial to the staff. The British Museum Print Room also furnished many riches, as we have seen.

"But it is the Bodleian Library at Oxford that provides the most vivid memories—the liveliness of fourteenth-century life in the spritely marginal sketches of *The Romance of Alexander*, and the seventeenth-century pageant in that greatest piece of all grangerizing, the *Burnet* and *Clarendon* in the Sutherland Collection. We trained ourselves to dash through one of those huge folios in six minutes, but never, never could we bring it down to five.

"The Bodleian folk are courtly, but they take no chances. A junior used to escort us through all the non-public rooms; we nicknamed it 'jailing'. My Uncle Herbert was once halted in a remote place downstairs; he was not one to stand by idly, and to his jailer's horror he grabbed a folio from the shelves. It proved to be a unique treasure; a book of drawings by Captain Wynne, that enigmatic Carolean architect. I always lose the reference, so some years the volume seems to vanish underground, but lately when I spoke to our invaluable old friend Strickland Gibson he said: 'Oh, yes, we've just had it out for an Oxford drawing; it's in my office now'.

"There were interesting experiences at the Bodleian in the last war. I went down on two days' leave in 1917, and mercifully wrote beforehand to explain matters; always an indispensable part of Oxford technique. I had run across Strickland Gibson as a sergeant in khaki, writing an elaborate analysis of German air organization at the Hotel Cecil, in a dismal little closet filled by an enormous cistern which dripped with unceasing fiendishness.

"When I arrived at the Bodleian I was interviewed by an elderly man who was new to me. He demanded sternly if I had been admitted a reader. I doubted if I had, but explained suavely that I had frequently 'read' there in past years, and he would find my name duly registered under H. Batsford (it would surely have been ultra-meticulous to state that my late uncle and I possessed the same single initial!). That was all right, and I passed muster.

"The naval commander who followed me did not fare so well. He was pink and plump, like a pleasant prize porker, and when similarly challenged said that he had not been formally admitted, but had come down on leave for research on the early history of his family places. 'No, I am not a member of this University,' he said, 'but I have the honour to hold His Majesty's commission as a ——'

" 'Oh, I don't know anything about that,' said the library representative. 'There are so many impostors about nowadays.' I gasped, for as a wavy two-striper I knew that any three-striper was a person of no small consequence, whom one invariably saluted.

"A similar experience long ago befell the late Earl of Buckinghamshire, a descendant of John Hampden. He had found two copies of an unknown pamphlet of a speech of the patriot, and, highly delighted, he had put them in his tailcoat pocket and gone off to present one to the Bodleian. His reception was discouraging. 'Well, sir, what do you want?' He was told that the Bodleian had everything about John Hampden, and that no such pamphlet existed. Drawing himself up to his full 6 ft. 6 in., the indignant peer slammed the papers down on the table and thundered, 'I am the Earl of Buckinghamshire, and I came to present you with a copy of this unknown speech, but since you have been so abominably and damnably rude, I will see you in hell first'. When the position was realized they were all over him, but he shook his head, grabbed the pamphlets and stalked forth.

"In this war the Bodleian carries on helpfully, unperturbed. We descend to the bowels of the earth, into a long tunnel under Broad Street, with a wire enclosure in which empty conveyers clank continuously to and fro, like the shaft-tunnel of some gargantuan vessel. In the new building a brisk, dapper little person received me the last time I was there. 'Yes,' he said reflectively, 'wartime makes queer bedfellows; we have strange libraries, stranger librarians, and strangest societies. Don't go into that room, or they will give you a blood transfusion before you can turn round, and keep out of that one, or you'll be plunged fathoms deep into statistics, and may not come to the surface for several days'."

XXVI

We have seen something of the character and methods of a publishing house during a century; from the time when young Bradley Thomas ventured into his first shop, to the contemporary circumstances of war. But there is another theme which I have not tackled because it is beyond my knowledge. Only Harry Batsford and his colleagues know the value of the friendships the firm has made during those years, and I leave it to them to contribute a chapter of notes on some of them.

AYMER VALLANCE, to whose work several references have occurred in this book, was an unusual and arresting figure, though his name is little known to the current generation. It is surprising that a member of a typical large Kentish family of country-house type should, from his days at Oriel College, Oxford, have developed on such individual lines. He became a fervent medievalist, with a passion for the art and architecture of the Middle Ages, a scholarly antiquarian, a lover of craftsmanship, a writer and lecturer. He was closely associated with William Morris on the side of his art-work—his bent was the reverse of socialistic—and he prepared the great account of Morris's work which appeared soon after his death. He could claim to have "discovered" Aubrey Beardsley and to have brought him into touch with John Lane; from this contact sprang the first drawings in *The Yellow Book* which caused such a sensation in their day. With the Batsfords, Vallance's connection extended over fifty years, as book collector, author, and shareholder. His folio on *The Old Colleges of Oxford* is a very full study; it appeared in 1912. In 1919 he produced an equally full survey of *Old Crosses and Lychgates;* but the publication of his exhaustive review of Belgium had to be abandoned owing to a sudden collapse in popular interest. Recently he prepared a detailed account of *English (Parish) Church Screens*, and the companion volume on the work of the Greater Churches was completed just before his death. There is no space here to tell of all his research and literary work. Stoneacre, the Tudor house which he acquired and inhabited for a time, in the parish of Otham in his native

Kent, was presented by him to the National Trust. He has passed from us while these pages are going through the press.

* * *

The long connection between LEWIS F. DAY and the Batsfords has already been touched on (p. 16), but some notice of the man himself and his work is desirable, since he was for thirty years prominent in art circles as designer, lecturer and writer. Though he never troubled to publicize himself or his work, he wielded a wide and varied influence in a quiet way. Day, unlike many artists of his time, took a sane, balanced view of the relations between art and commerce, and was emphatic on adapt-ing design to the technical conditions of industrial pro-cesses. He was Master of the Artworkers' Guild and also director of a Manchester cotton firm. His views are set down in an interesting tilting discussion with Walter Crane, who, red and rebel-lious, railed at commerce while doing well out of it. They used postcards as mis-siles, and the exchanges were

A Caricature by Crane of the Lewis F. Day-Walter Crane discussions. From *Moot Points* (1903).

published in an interesting little shilling book, *Moot Points*, 1903; one of Crane's illustrative caricatures is reproduced.

Day had intense and catholic appreciation of all forms of craftsmanship, acquired in many years' wanderings over the old cities of Europe before they were injured by later nine-teenth-century changes. These travels also furnished material for his survey of stained glass, *Windows*.

* * *

Among our oldest friends is ARTHUR STRATTON, who has been associated with the firm for forty-five years, as draughts-man, author, editor and tried adviser. Our shelves are the richer for his books on Wren Churches, Elements of Classic Architecture, the Orders, and others. But his greatest work is the study of Tudor Domestic Architecture, which he pre-pared with Herbert Batsford, and with it ranks his fine review of *The English Interior*. Arthur Stratton has the generous heart which warms scholarship and keeps it human. One sign of this was the appreciation he showed of our firm by proposing my election as an Honorary Associate of the Royal Institute of British Architects.

He prepared for us a series of large diagrams of English Architectural Styles, which I still consider to be one of the best forms of primary architectural education. But they have been a sales disappointment, although the handbooks which he wrote to go with them are decidedly popular.

When we first knew Arthur Stratton he was a firmly settled Londoner. But now he has discovered the country, and his heart has magnified itself now that he is transplanted near to the western Sussex Downs.

* * *

Perhaps the purest piece of English literature Batsfords have ever published is WILLIAM HENRY WARD's *French Renaissance Architecture*. He was a brilliant scholar-architect of a type not often found nowadays, and his wide historical knowledge was wedded to a remarkable facility for languages. His French was perfect and his Italian fluent; he also taught himself to read Dutch. His standard work, which I have mentioned, beautifully written and informed with immaculate taste, is still in print after thirty years. He also edited the selection of Du Cerceau's drawings, *French Châteaux and Gardens*, published in 1909. He worked for us on a book on North-East France, with the collaboration and drawings of Sydney R. Jones, which we dearly wished to publish. But the later unpopularity of the subject of the 1914 war forced us to abandon it, along with the similar book on Belgium by Aymer Vallance. We have seen how Ward saw service in the last war. As a result of it he died, a middle-aged man, in 1924.

Ward had a dry and penetrating sense of humour. When he brought us his manuscript of *French Renaissance Architecture* we were terrified by its length, so we asked Phené Spiers to advise us.

"You *must* cut it down," said the old man, grimly, to Ward, who reluctantly tried to do as he was told.

But he had his riposte. When Spiers' new edition of *Greece and Rome* was published Uncle Herbert found Ward in the British Museum, almost hidden by a mass of classical reference books. In the next number of the *R.I.B.A. Journal* appeared a review of Spiers' book in which Ward pointed out, in fine classical English, some two hundred and twenty slips and misprints; a depressing total for any scholar.

Ward lived in an Adam house in Bedford Square, which he shared with an architect friend. It was beautifully furnished, and it was a pleasure to go there and enjoy the scholarship and modesty of a man whose mind was as fine as his prose.

* * *

There is one story which tells all, of our connection with A. E. RICHARDSON, R.A., for twenty years Professor of Architecture at University College. His association with us has extended over thirty years, but this incident suffices to show that argument and respect may well go hand in hand.

Uncle Herbert could be crotchety with his authors. He often gave Richardson a gruelling time, especially when he was writing the text of the great *Monumental Classic Architecture*, of which the introduction was a difficult piece of work. The author would bring in the draft, only to find Uncle Herbert in a fractious mood. "Take the wretched stuff away, re-write it and make it more readable," he would say. Why Richardson put up with this is more than I can say; but his devotion to his work was greater than any petty pride and he stuck it out. The hammering went on for months until the book saw the light of day.

Shortly afterwards Richardson was having tea with another architect and was heard to say: "I think I'll ask Herbert to give me another book to do".

"Good heavens, man," said his companion, "don't be such an idiot! Think how he's browbeaten and badgered you for months. You mustn't think of it."

"Oh, I don't know," said Richardson. "After all, it's rather cold out of hell."

Richardson combines whimsical humour with an unrivalled knowledge and intense appreciation of eighteenth-century architecture and craftsmanship. He showed this when at the end of the last war he bought a late eighteenth-century house, with a small park, at Ampthill. The house was designed by Henry Holland, Richardson's favourite architect and æsthetic hero. With equal scholarship and taste he filled the place, which is called Avenue House, with furniture and fittings of the period. Unlike most consciously period houses it is not oppressive or inhuman; it contains the spirit as well as the craftsmanship of the century.

At Ampthill Richardson loves to dress himself and his guests in eighteenth-century clothes, with wigs and church-warden pipes, and to dine with complete Georgian fittings. He used on occasions to call at a friend's house carried in his sedan-chair by two men in correct chairmen's costumes.

The local policeman once appeared and said: "I shall have to report you, sir, for not showing a light."

Richardson knows the laws of this century as well as the spirit of the eighteenth. He answered: "Oh no, you can't do that. This is not a wheeled vehicle".

But he is no antiquarian pedant, and he ranges all over the country by car and train. The journey to and from Ampthill used often to be a long and penitential pilgrimage, with a windy wait at Luton. Richardson wrote repeatedly to the authorities: "Dear Midland Railway, can't you let us poor people at Ampthill have a nice express all to ourselves? Do, please, and we shall always love you. From your affectionate passenger, A. E. Richardson, f.s.a., f.r.i.b.a., Professor of Architecture, University College, London".

The Railway Company at last sent a representative to say this sort of nonsense must stop. But Richardson got his express.

His driving is like that of Jehu, the son of Nimshi. He is never happy at less than fifty miles an hour, though this frequently rises to seventy when he finds himself on the long deserted roads of the open country towards Cambridge. To travel around with him is a liberal education: to see the churches he has tenderly repaired, the forgotten tiny hamlets, and the remote country houses. One Sunday Charles Fry and I were driving with him when we came upon the well-proportioned brown stone church of Eaton Socon. That same evening it was gutted by fire. It was like Richardson to make the gesture immediately . . . of designing for it a complete set of quietly appropriate new fittings. I remember, too, a day at St. Neots, with its old inns and magnificent Perpendicular tower and fabric. Richardson lured us into the junk shops, and found butter stamps to add to his collection of old household gear. But even more pleasant was our switchback run down the lanes, with broad green verges, to Keysoe, with its windmill, and to Pertenhall, where we wandered over the large late-Georgian rectory, lovely and deserted, with only a leaden pump in the scullery for water supply and a chaste Georgian temple in the grounds for sanitary convenience. Then to Kimbolton, with Vanbrugh's great four-square mansion, and the pleasant irregular houses colour-washed in shades of orange and decorated with painted *treillage*.

I remember most of all, among the delicious, unknown, rural country of Huntingdonshire, the day we went with Richardson to Bushmead Priory. The way turned into a little park of old gnarled oaks and hundreds of scurrying rabbits, to a red-brick, mid-Georgian house, and a kindly welcome from Mr. and Mrs. Wade-Geary. In an octagonal room with Canaletto paintings were divine Chippendale chairs with contemporary needlework coverings, and outside a large aviary filled with whirring budgerigars. Behind was the fifteenth-century refectory of the priory itself; and the original illuminated service books were kept in the house, having, in strange, rare fashion, never been moved from the place where they were in use five centuries before. We fingered a few Greek coins of the Roman Occupation, which had been unearthed from a field near by, carrying the human tide back more than fifteen hundred years.

* * *

It is impossible to mention all of the circle of stalwarts among authors who worked with the uncles in late Victorian days, but they included a number of notable figures who deserve more than brief reference. The long-reaching connection with J. ALFRED GOTCH, PP.R.I.B.A., of Kettering, has been referred to; he had a rare faculty for expressing the results of close research in a lucid and informative narrative. Though primarily interested in the Early Renaissance, he established the position of John Webb by close keen study of the Inigo Jones drawings, and his *English Home* is a valuable survey of Later Renaissance domestic design in exteriors, interiors, plaster and ironwork. JOHN BELCHER, R.A., who sponsored the folio *Later Renaissance Architecture*, genial, agreeable, bearded and spectacled, was an outstanding instance of an architect who added authorship to a wide and highly success-ful practice; he also wrote an attractive little book for general readers, *Essentials in Architecture*. His collaborator, MERVYN

MACARTNEY, edited the *English Houses and Gardens*, of engraved historic views. He was for long connected with *The Architectural Review* and was surveyor to St. Paul's during the successful efforts for its preservation. With them must be ranked GEORGE H. BIRCH, F.S.A., author of *London City Churches*, with collotype plates from Latham's photographs. He was an antiquary and lover of old London, and was for years curator of the Soane Museum—a massive, picturesque figure in his black skull cap, with the beloved cat he called his white angel. But it was a black Persian that sat on his pillow during his last illness.

A friend of many years' standing was A. N. PRENTICE, designer of charming houses and exquisite draughtsman. His *Renaissance Architecture and Ornament in Spain*, 1894, was particularly popular in the United States, where it achieved the distinction of more than one pirated edition. As a shareholder he was a regular figure at the Company's general meetings until he was recently taken from us. Another distinguished domestic architect who was an able author was E. GUY DAWBER, who prepared the Kent and Sussex, and Cotswold volumes in the *Regional Cottage Series*, illustrated by Davie's photographs. He will be remembered for his work in founding the Council for the Preservation of Rural England, for which he was knighted. Other architect-authors who contributed to this series, both successful designers and able draughtsmen, were W. CURTIS GREEN, R.A., and BASIL OLIVER, F.R.I.B.A., who also has to his credit a general review of *Old Cottages*, which appeared in 1929. H. INIGO TRIGGS had a specialized interest in historic gardens, and as we have seen was responsible for *Formal Gardens in England and Scotland*. Owing to Bradley Batsford's illness, this parallel study of *Italian Gardens* was published elsewhere. His *Garden Craft in Europe* is an extensive and valuable review, but the projected account of French Gardens was never completed, for he suffered from chronic ill-health and died comparatively young. Triggs was an early pioneer of Town Planning, and staggered the R.I.B.A. by asking that a grant he won should be devoted to a study of this unheard-of subject. WALTER GODFREY, F.S.A., architect, antiquary and historical scholar, has worked with the Batsford firm for thirty-five years, and his varied output includes *A History of Architecture in London*, *The English Staircase*, *Mural Monuments* and a two-part *Story of Architecture in England.* He is now Director of the National Buildings Record. *Longo intervallo* in the same antiquarian field is EDMUND VALE, whose Batsford record is equally varied, with, among others, *How to Look at Old Buildings, Ancient England* and *Curiosities of Town and Countryside.* The two latter were seen through the press while he was in three-starred khaki.

*   *   *

A glance has been taken at the work of THE QUENNELLS, who were in themselves a pair of intensely interesting personalities. That a successful architect and his artist wife, with a growing family, should strike out a new literary line in history in their middle forties was in itself a surprising development. Previously C. H. B. Quennell had written a little *Handbook on Norwich Cathedral* and a book on his own *Modern Suburban Houses;* but in the fifteen years after the Armistice he and his wife produced a dozen books which have transformed history teaching, and are as alive as ever in their influence and popularity to-day, both here and in America.

C. H. B. Quennell was a sort of literary Escoffier; he could make of a prehistoric period or a medieval century a tasty, nourishing dish, well flavoured and attractively garnished, good to look at and to sample. He kept in middle life much of his youthfulness and an abounding and whimsical humour, with successive enthusiasms in sudden spate. His intense feeling and love for craftsmanship and its workers were abiding and constant, but were curiously married to a keenness to explore mechanical processes—he wanted to know, and make you see, how the steam engine originated, how the spinning jenny and seed-drill worked, and his interest could spread itself over most forms of human development. Later he was strangely gripped by an overwhelming passion for the life and work of Ancient Greece, far beyond the sphere where the English public could respond, and this was followed by an intense attraction for the work of William Morris, Rossetti and Burne-Jones.

It was a pleasurable excitement to work for and with him, even if his lighthearted sunniness was shot with occasional showers of lively controversy. After his death in 1935, Marjorie Quennell found a congenial and successful post as curator of the L.C.C. Geffrye Museum, Kingsland Road, and the grimy slum urchins of Shoreditch loved with her encouragement to come in droves to draw its old furniture, pottery, glass and metalwork. After a serious illness she has gone to the United States, where she has actively taken up the work of illustrating a series of books on history and geography, to the joy of friendly publishing firms. But we shall be glad to see her bright personality among us again.

Later the firm collaborated with a pair of enthusiastic teachers, DOROTHY HARTLEY and MADGE ELLIOT, in producing a series of six historical books, covering the Conquest to the eighteenth century, with illustrations from contemporary manuscripts, drawings and prints. Their research was unwearying, and the series was great fun to do. Its results to us and to a fairly wide circle were stimulating, instructive and informative, but the curious aloofness of the English race to many forms of the graphic arts came decidedly into play, and it was found that teachers especially were far less attracted by medieval manuscripts and eighteenth-century engravings than by the Quennells' drawn version of such material; they preferred their stuff predigested. Consequently this *Life and Work of the English People* never became as well known or appreciated as the *Everyday Things* and *Everyday Life Series*. Uncle Herbert experienced a similar disappointment with his well-schemed oblong album of views of country houses and gardens reproduced from Kip's engravings and similar sources.

Dorothy Hartley adds to her keenness for the Middle Ages an informed love of country life and work; she has contributed *The Countryman's England* to the *Heritage Series*, as well as other country books and a study of medieval costume. Madge Elliot has written for other firms a series of volumes on English social history and a batch of successful playlets.

Space limits preclude reference to a number of authors who have written on the teaching of decorative and fine art, but we cannot omit mention of the cheery, humorous friendliness of ALLEN W. SEABY, now in retirement after a long career as Professor of Fine Art in the University of Reading. His work on *Drawing for Art Students* has been through two editions; his version of the Trajan Column lettering Professor Seaby cut in wood by his own hand. If his series of four little volumes on *Art in the Life of Mankind* has had a disappointing reception, that may be set down to the national indifference to most forms of art outside the narrative-pictorial. Professor Seaby, as a shareholder, is still keenly interested in the work of the firm. Miss D. D. SAWER scored a decided success with her *Everyday Art at School and Home;* this has been followed by a sequel: *Art in Daily Life for Young and Old.* She has also contributed popular little manuals on *Sketching* and *Perspective.*

* * *

Charles Fry has already given a picture of SIR REGINALD BLOMFIELD coming into our offices during the Blitz, to see his proofs; an old man, full of learning and courage. He has since died, and he died our friend. But it was not always so, for our final association was preceded by skirmishes which lasted for fifteen years. In 1897 he brought out his *History of Renaissance Architecture in England,* in two handsome volumes, while our Belcher and Macartney's book of large plates, *Later Renaissance Architecture,* was in course of publication. Our firm issued Gotch's *Early Renaissance Architecture in England* four years later. Although it covered only the Early period, Blomfield scented a possible rival for his big work, so he published a compact octavo edition of his £2 10s. book for seven shillings and sixpence; a marvel of condensation and cheapness.

We replied by stating, in advertising Gotch's work, "No cheaper edition of this book can ever be issued". (Actually we reduced it from one guinea to fifteen shillings when we published a new edition in 1914.) That was our first small rivalry with Blomfield. Later the firm published W. H. Ward's book on *French Renaissance Architecture.* Blomfield paralleled it with two volumes on the subject, covering it to 1625, followed by two more on the later styles. The books treated a great subject and there was room for all of them.

The exchanges went on. In 1902 Batsfords announced Inigo Triggs' folio, *Formal Gardens in England and Scotland,* an ambitious work in three parts, at one guinea each. The book was to be sold by subscription. This brought an indignant letter from Blomfield asserting that his *Formal Garden in England* (1892, 7/6) was *the* book on the subject and demanding a change in our title. He added a postscript: "Be good enough to inform me what alteration you will make". My uncles were dealing with the matter, and they were the equals of Blomfield. They wrote him that they were aware of his excellent little pioneer book, which they sold, but that they could not admit his sole right to the words "Formal Garden". Back came an angry flash: "I have received your impertinent letter and shall immediately go and see my solicitor".

My uncles sat back and smiled. By hunting back, they found that the term *Formal Garden* had been used in Sir Uvedale Price's *On the Picturesque*, published in 1794. So that contest ended.

But Blomfield still had one more shot in his locker. Shortly after there appeared a virulent review in an important literary journal referring to our new venture. The reviewer wrote: "These photographic views accumulate somehow, we suppose, and therefore they have to be published. Hence some form of flimsy introduction is tacked on to them, and they are given forth to the world".

My uncles were convinced that this was due to some reviewer friend of Blomfield, and I urged them to start a libel action against the journal. But they were wiser than I was.

It is a strange and rather endearing aspect of publishing that we should enjoy these battles and yet allow friendship to be born of them.

Some forty years later, on publishing Blomfield's book on Norman Shaw, I told him how pleased I was that the tiffs with the uncles were wiped from the slate. All that Sir Reginald answered was, "Did I have tiffs with them? Well, my memory is far from a long one, and they have completely gone from it".

* * *

The name of SYDNEY JONES has been mentioned more than once already, but mention is not enough. He has been our friend for thirty-five years. In Herbert Batsford's time he prepared the drawings for *The English Village* and *The English Manor House;* the text of both of these was written by the late Reverend P. H. Ditchfield. After the war Jones gave to the public a sample of his unrivalled knowledge of the country in *Touring England,* a compact little handbook of carefully chosen routes. He has since contributed *English Village Homes* to the *Heritage Series,* and a new revision of Gertrude Jekyll's *Household Life* (page 132); but the quires of both were wiped out in the Blitz.

Sydney Jones shares our love of the English countryside, and he is a persistent rambler; we have wandered together over much of England. He loves the land and he hates motor-cars; an odd amusement to his friends on *The Autocar,* to which he is the oldest contributor. His latest success is with *London Triumphant*.

*   *   *

My uncles had great faith in the scholarship of women, believing in their rare patience and concentration in the gathering and collating of details from the welter of history. One of these was ELEANOR ROWE, a great friend of theirs. Her range of wood-carving books is extensive and varied. There were other wood-carving ladies who worked for us, and an embroidery group which includes Grace Christie, Louisa F. Pesel, Ann Brandon-Jones and Winifred M. Clark.

Our longest connection with a woman writer is with MARGARET JOURDAIN. I have one recollection of her which stands apart from the thirty-five years of serious work she has done for us. We have mentioned Richardson's passion for the eighteenth century and his delight in wearing its dress. Sometimes he affected Regency costume, in memory of his idol, Henry Holland. One day when he went to the R.I.B.A. dressed like this, he ran into Margaret Jourdain, whose knowledge of eighteenth-century furniture and habits rivals his own. He invited her to accompany him down Regent Street; they walked arm in arm. Her sense of humour was equal to the occasion, but she confessed afterwards that she wondered if the people in the street imagined them to be a novel form of advertisement for Johnnie Walker Whisky.

Miss Jourdain's first book with us was *Old Lace*, published in 1908. We have already mentioned that she collaborated with Colonel Mulliner on *The Library of Decorative Art*, and later completed the series. She also wrote a work on simple English Interiors, followed by a thorough study of *English Plaster Work, 1500-1800*. Miss Jourdain delights in unearthing the names and careers of craftsmen of decoration and furniture in wood, plaster and metal during the three hundred years covered by her books. For many years she has lived with Miss Ivy Compton Burnett, whose psychological novels are so much admired by the younger school.

*   *   *

About the middle of the 1920's it occurred to the firm that GERTRUDE JEKYLL's *Old West Surrey*, with its intimate survey of a vanished country life, could be expanded into a review covering generally the old household life of England. The suggestion appealed to Miss Jekyll, and we made still another friend: a friendship particularly pleasing to me, because it meant that I could visit her at Munstead Wood, beyond Godalming. I liked walking through the branching, hilly, sandy Surrey lanes, to her pleasant little secluded house, right in size and spirit, surrounded by gardens which shaded into the untouched woodland. How pleased she was, and how pleased she could make her visitor, as she showed her rare Siberian heaths, and the great yew which a touch of deft clipping had turned into a giant cat, kneeling on its paws!

Gertrude Jekyll was quite old then, and sometimes she was unequal to an interview. On other days she would enter into the plan with lively zest. Nicholson's life-like portrait of her in the Tate shows exactly what she looked like. She finished the book and it was well received. After she was dead we asked Sydney Jones to enlarge and re-illustrate it for the *British Heritage Series*. Thus her book appeared in three versions over a period of thirty years. When it is reprinted after the war, which it will be, it will be making its fourth appearance.

DOREEN WALLACE is another distinguished addition to our list. Her regional books on East Anglia and the Lakeland are attractive and knowledgeable studies, and she has also written on *How to Grow Food* for the *Home Front Handbooks*. A nice printer's error crept into this last work. The proof came to us entitled *How to Grow Good*. We remembered the failure of our *Fellowship Series* on such high-minded affairs, and author and publisher smiled. Doreen Wallace is no mild creature with her pen, and she stirs up many a skirmish with her vigorous views. She wrote something rather outspoken about a new building at Walsingham, and a reprint and public apology were demanded. The passage was modified, but I cannot imagine Doreen Wallace making an apology for anything. She was equally emphatic about Barrow-in-Furness, and an ex-mayor was most vehement. In her bright little Home Gardening book she attacked predatory birds and recommended drastic treatment for them . . . from the gardener's point of view. This time the bird lovers fell about her head. We altered the passage in the cause of peace.

Doreen Wallace lives in a yellow-plastered, Georgian-fronted, Tudor manor-farm near Diss. She is a fighter in all things, especially against tithes. When I last went to see her there had been a forced sale, and a black patch on the lawn showed where she had hanged the Tithe Act from a gallows and then burned it, in front of her house, upon which she had hung the slogans: *Foreign Farmers Pay No Tithes. The Church's Motto: Come Unto Me Ye Weary And I Will Sell You Up.*

Among other women authors who have recently worked with the firm is CHRISTINA HOLE, of Oxford. She has already contributed three books to our lists; there is a fourth in the press and another to follow. Her *English Folklore* was followed by a collection of stories of English ghost-lore, under the title *Haunted England.* Then came a review of *English Customs and Ceremonies.* Christina Hole possesses in a remarkable degree the faculty of reviewing a complex subject over a number of centuries, clearly and analytically. To her scholarship is added a mordant wit.

*   *   *

The variety of callers during the years at High Holborn has already been indicated. But the story up to now has been mainly concerned with the publishing side. If the century's customers in both Holborn and Mayfair could be assembled they would make a large gathering, interesting in many ways, whether in appearance, costume, vocation, or literary tastes. There is no space to recall many of those vanished figures, but some typical names may be seen in the extract from a List of Subscribers reproduced on page 75. Here, however, is a sketch of one of the old school, who continued as one of our customers until only the other day.

He was a customer of long standing, an elderly gentleman of immaculate appearance, stiff as a ramrod, who seemed to bring with him a redolence of the Edwardian age. He was dressed in a long drainpipe overcoat and a bowler-hat with a marvellous curling brim; in his button-hole was often a bunch of violets, and in his hands lavender gloves and an irreproachably folded umbrella. His passion was for the engraved decorative books of the eighteenth century: designs for ironwork, furniture, and so on. He had amassed a large library of these works, which was unfortunately dispersed after his death.

This well-to-do bachelor would arrive in either a splendidly varnished brougham or a high, antique Rolls-Royce embellished to suit his taste. French ormolu coach handles replaced the serviceable standard pattern, and a remarkable glass erection in the roof provided ventilation without window draughts. On these occasions his plump old coachman discarded his cockaded top hat and livery to appear as surely one of the most elderly of chauffeurs. Either of these equipages would cause such a stir in Holborn, and later in North Audley Street, that small crowds would gather to inspect them. The coachman's disdain for errand-boys' banter was impressive.

Curiously, this elderly figure was only a few years predeceased by his mother. From her death until after his own the family hatchment, lozenge-shaped and bearing their arms within a sable mourning border, was displayed over the portico of the gloomy old house in the gloomy old square where they had lived together.

*   *   *

Among friends of Batsfords we have spoken of some authors, and of others who have vied with them in the closeness as in the length and friendliness of their association. But this chapter would be incomplete without some mention of the representatives of American publishers, and we must include two or three figures from the assortment who have impinged on the firm in its century.

Batsfords enjoy established relations with a number of friendly American publishers, but their chief associates for the last fifty years have been Scribners. Charles Fry has mentioned how he has mingled with them in New York, but the majority of the work goes through the London representative, a post wisely and pleasantly filled since the last war by Charles Kingsley, with whom Batsfords' relations have always been of the most cordial friendliness, in the charming old Adam house in Bedford Square which he arranged for them to occupy. If Charles Kingsley's recall to America in 1940 still leaves a feeling of loss, it is good to know that he has been enjoying a well-deserved rest after his long exile. All at Batsfords look forward to his return.

Until 1922, Scribners' representative for many years was a remarkable figure, Lemuel W. Bangs—a little, dapper, elderly man, with the complete turn-out of a late-Victorian dandy. (There is a lady in England who still inserts a memorial notice in the newspapers on the anniversary of his death.) He was the least American Yankee that could be imagined; his office was a room at Dawsons in Breams Buildings, and he had no staff at all—Dawsons did all his clerical work, but he wrote his brief notes in his own hand. There is no need to dismiss his methods as prehistoric; they were devised with almost Chinese cunning and ingenuity. No man ever transacted a greater volume of business with less trouble to himself or less outlay in working expenses to his firm. He spent the morning at his Club and never got to his office until after lunch. If you wanted an order, it was best to call at half-past five. He had an intense aversion to long letters, which Uncle Herbert loved writing. "Damn him, here's another of 'em," he would say, flourishing the closely type-written sheets at me when I dropped in to try to extract an order. Then: "But he's the son of his father, and I suppose I must take some copies; put me down for 250".

From Lippincotts of Philadelphia would come, most Januarys, Jack Jefferson Jones, cheery, shrewd and humorous. It is sad to think that his bright presence will be seen no more, for he died after a brief illness in 1941. He would take books from us over which some of his folk on the other side would shake their heads; but success usually justified his judgment.

Jefferson Jones never knew the summer beauty of England, for he invariably turned up in midwinter; but he always longed to look at the Cotswolds. It is difficult for Americans on business trips to disentangle themselves, but at last he arrived in March, and a day was fixed when he, Sydney Jones and myself drove through Abingdon and Witney, to lunch at Burford, then up over the Wolds and by the Dikler Valley to Bourton-on-the-Water and the escarpment edge. That fresh, early spring day, with its fleeting sunlight and scurrying white clouds, will always live in my memory. Now some of the quiet fields are busy aerodromes, and we did not know then that it was Jefferson Jones' last sight of the old country.

Some years, Jo Lippincott himself would arrive instead. It was long before it was discovered that he was also a successful author of children's nature books, and on this account we were keen that he should meet Frances Pitt, as he was himself. So one Sunday Brian Cook drove him, Fry and myself to lunch at Evesham and to have tea with Miss Pitt at the pleasant old house above the Severn woods beyond Bridgnorth. Then we returned through Ludlow and Leominster to Tewkesbury for the night. But the shadow of Munich hung over the land, and Lippincott was anxious to get back. So when we came to old stone Painswick he telephoned his London office and the manager dashed off to secure a bathroom in the *Queen Mary* for fifty pounds. The way onwards led past ideal Owlpen manor-house, through Malmesbury and Shaftesbury, for a late lunch with Cecil Beaton at Ashcombe. There, as we have seen, Beaton has found his ideal house deep below the highest point of Cranborne Chase. The eighteenth-century mansion has vanished and only a green lawn marks its site. But the red brick orangery makes an ideal studio and the bailiff's house a compact little residence. As we sped back from Salisbury to London, war seemed impending. When we said good-bye to Jo in the Haymarket, a lorry laden with gas cylinders clattered down the hill. Doubtless it was to replenish the barrage balloons, but he groaned, "Gosh, here comes the poison gas!" and turned sorrowfully away. He sent me a bottle of very old brandy as a farewell gift, but before the *Queen Mary* saw the Statue of Liberty the crisis was over, and our last year of respite had begun.

* * *

I have written of our friends who come to see us. But this is not enough. On looking back through this book, I find many references to the members of our staff, but none which expresses the fullness of our gratitude to them. War sets a strange test upon loyalty; it either addles the nerves of those who work for one or it intensifies their devotion. Perhaps we have been clever or fortunate in choosing and keeping our staff. I only know that the anxiety of these past four years has been halved by the cheerful way in which they have given their hearts and talents to the struggles.

A publishing house of any standing and length of life owes much to its senior staff. Of these, my mind turns immediately to Alexander John Green, senior accountant for thirty-seven years, and Secretary of the Company for twenty of the thirty years of its existence. He is a glutton for work, devoted and loyal and, what Batsfords always like in their staff, endowed with a sense of humour. Green has his side-line of interest, for he is devoted to organs and organ recitals, and will cheerfully run up to Liverpool for the day to hear some celebrated player.

For over sixteen years the all-important position of production manager at Batsfords has been filled by Francis Lucarotti, who has outstandingly the first-line qualifications:

35.   Alexander John Green, Secretary and Chief Accountant.

40. The Regency Building in High Holborn, first occupied by Day & Martin's Blacking, of which No. 94 (a slice of which is seen on the extreme right) formed a part.

From an engraving by T. H. Shepherd.

41. High Holborn in the 'Eighties. Batsfords' earlier premises at No. 52 are the second house from the left.

he is a super-wizard on figures, and can perform miracles on paper stocks like Elijah with the widow's cruse. He unites a cheery and patient disposition with a quick sense of humour, and has a trustful and optimistic bent which can occasionally even prove embarrassing. The garbled versions of his name which come to hand in correspondence are innumerable and never ending—it would be amusing to make a collection of them.

Girls first joined the firm in 1916. The senior lady is now Marjorie Bryning, who as a shy, quiet girl, not long from India, first came to us early in 1924. She has long been secretary to the Directors, involving all the trade publicity and the review department. Her complete switchover to the sphere of country orders has already been mentioned, and her hillside, single-roomed dwelling at Malvern is also a self-denial, for if she rejoices in it, there is always its distance from her family.

Some of the later additions to the staff have already proved their worth and they fill well-established positions. On the retail side, Maureen Boland, one of our four girl workers with the initials M.B., has shown her many-sided usefulness, especially in her tact, patience and resourcefulness in dealing with customers. T. H. Payne, who for years has specialized in foreign books, is active and capable in showing our publications to the trade of the London district and in building up a solid connection with them. Thomas Burrows, who was long with the firm of Parsons of Brompton Road, has consolidated and expanded the secondhand side in association with Hanneford-Smith; to their joint credit is a series of fine illustrated catalogues issued once again after an interval of many years. F. Finnissy, who has been with the firm for many years, is as reliable as he is actively industrious in the key position of stock-keeper and chief packer.

XXVII

This narrative has changed hands so often during the writing of this book that I hope that the reader will not be confused in unravelling the pieces that belong to Harry Batsford, Charles Fry, or myself as editor. Our chief difficulty has been that its preparation has given us so much pleasure

INDEX